Microsoft
PowerPoint 2016 Basics

by

Saritha Bathini

For Technical support, send us an email to
sarithatutorialbooks@gmail.com

Contents

Chapter 1: Getting Started with Microsoft PowerPoint 2016

Microsoft PowerPoint 2016 is a creative and innovation application that is used to develop a professional presentation to deliver it to the audience. Microsoft PowerPoint 2016 has various uses. Some of them are listed below.

- You can present your ideas, product, proposal, or organization with professionally designed and organized slides.
- You can elaborate a bulleted point using pictures, shapes, and WordArt.
- This application has tools to show and explain an idea using various types of diagrams such as hierarchies, process diagrams, pyramids, and so on.
- You can present a numeric data using Charts and Tables.
- You can make your presentation look good by using various styles, color themes, effects, and other formatting options.
- You can also create a template with customized color themes, designs, and layouts. This will help you to show your brand image.
- You can review a presentation by adding and receiving comments from a team. This will help you to create a best quality presentation.

Starting PowerPoint 2016

To start **Microsoft PowerPoint 2016** in Windows 8 or 8.1, click the Windows icon on the bottom left corner, and then click the down arrow located at the bottom left corner; the Apps grid appears. On the Apps grid, click the PowerPoint 2016  icon; the Backstage View of **PowerPoint 2016** appears.

To start Microsoft PowerPoint 2016 in Windows 10, type 'powerpoint' in the search box located on the task bar. Select **PowerPoint 2016** from the results.

Note: *If you are working in Windows 7, click the start menu icon at the bottom left corner to open the Start Menu. Enter PowerPoint 2016 in the search bar available on the Start Menu, and then click on the PowerPoint 2016 icon.*

Creating a New Presentation

You can create a new presentation from the start screen of the PowerPoint window or from the Backstage View. You can use the predesigned templates which save time and helps to design a professional presentation.

To start a blank presentation:

1. Click the **File** tab.

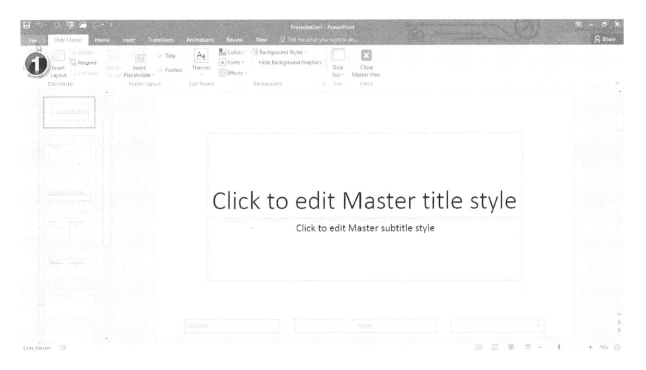

2. Click the **New** option on the **File** menu.

Various templates under many categories such as Presentation, Business, Orientation, Education, Blue, and so on are displayed on the backstage view. You can also enter a keyword in the Search bar available at the top, and find various templates available online. Click the **Pushpin** button to pin the selected template to the list.

3. Select a presentation template of your choice (or) select the Blank presentation template. A dialog box with the preview of the selected template appears.

4. Select a color scheme from the dialog; the preview appears.

5. Click the Back or Forward buttons to view the other slide layouts from the selected template.

6. Click the Back 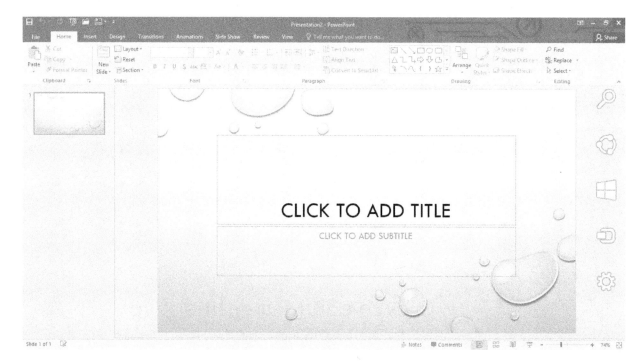 or Forward buttons to view the other templates.

7. Click the **Create** button to create. PowerPoint creates a presentation from the selected template.

Opening an Existing Presentation

After creating a presentation and saving it, you may need to open it to edit or present the slide show. You can open an existing presentation by using **Open** dialog box. The easiest way to open an existing presentation is to find it in the Recent Presentation list in the Backstage View.

Follow the steps given next to open an existing presentation.

1. Click the **File** tab to display the Backstage View.

2. Click the **Open** button.
3. Click **Recent**.
   A. The Recent Presentation list appears.

B. The list is divided into categories like Today, Yesterday, Last Week, Older along with the date and time you used it.

C. You can pin the presentation to the list by clicking on Pushpin button.

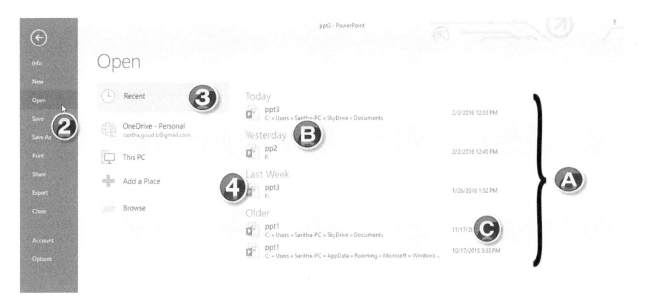

4. Select a presentation from the list.

(or)

5. Click **This PC** , if you do not find the presentation in the list; a list of recently used folders appears.

6. Browse to the location of the presentation by selecting the required folder.

7. Select the presentation file.

(or)

8. Click the **Browse** button; PowerPoint displays the **Open** dialog box.

9. Select the folder containing the presentation.

10. Select the presentation file.

11. Click the **Open** button; PowerPoint opens the selected presentation.

User Interface

To design a presentation and present a slide show, you need to find all the commands and options. The user interface of PowerPoint 2016 helps you to easily access all the commands and options. The main component of the user interface is the ribbon. It has all the commands that are used to design a presentation.

The ribbon is arranged in a hierarchy of tabs, groups, and commands. Groups such as **Clipboard**, **Slides**, and **Font** consist of commands which are grouped based on their usage. Some groups include a drop down arrow buttons to display the gallery of commands or menus. Groups in turn are grouped into various tabs. For example, the groups such as **Clipboard**, **Slides**, are **Font** are located in the **Home** tab.

Various components of the PowerPoint 2016 User Interface are shown in figure.

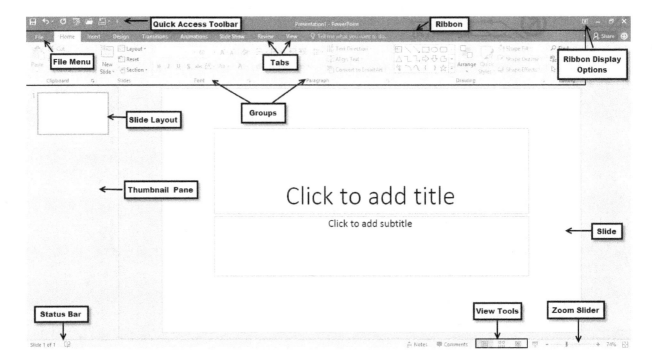

Quick Access Toolbar

The **Quick Access Toolbar** has some commonly used commands such as **New, Open, Save, Undo, Redo, Regenerate,** and so on. You can add more commands to the **Quick Access Toolbar** by clicking on the down-arrow next to it, and then selecting commands from the drop-down menu. You can also use the **More Commands** option located on the drop-down menu and add new commands from the **PowerPoint Options** dialog.

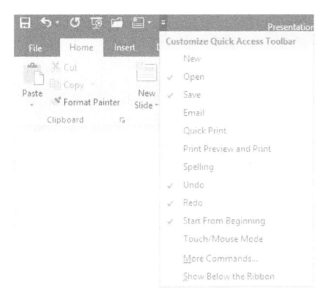

File Menu

The File Menu appears when you click the **FILE** tab located at the top left corner of the window. The **File Menu** has a list of self-explanatory menus. You can start a new file, open an existing file, save, print, share, export, and close files using the File Menu. click **Options** on the File Menu to open the **Options** dialog.

The **General** page of the **Options** dialog shows the options related to the user interface, office theme, personalization and, Startup options.

The **Proofing** page shows the spelling, grammar, and AutoCorrect options.

The **Save** page shows the options to set the file format, auto recovery settings, server files location, and embed font settings.

The **Language** page shows the options to set the language preferences.

The **Advanced** page shows the editing, cut/copy/paste, image size and quality, chart, display, slide show, print settings, and general options.

The **Customize Ribbon** page allows you to add or remove commands from the Ribbon. To add a command to a particular group of a ribbon tab, select the command from the left side section. Next, expand the ribbon tab from the right side section, and then select the group. click the **Add** button to add the command.

The **Quick Access Toolbar** page allows you to add or remove commands from the Quick Access Toolbar. The **Add-Ins** page displays the plug-ins added to PowerPoint. You can manage plug-ins by clicking the **Go** button located at the bottom.

The **Trust Center** page shows the options related to the file security. You can click the **Trust Center Settings** button to define the security settings.

Click **OK** on the **PowerPoint Options** dialog to apply the changes.

The Ribbon

The ribbon appears at the top of the window. It has various tabs. When you click on a tab, different groups appear. These groups show commands on them.

Various tabs available on the ribbon are given next.

Home tab

This tab has commands to add new slides and edit text data. Also, it has commands to draw shapes, format, find, and replace text data.

Insert tab

This tab has commands to insert objects into the slide. You can insert new slides using the **Slides** group. The **Tables** group allows you to insert tables into the slide. The **Image** group allows you to insert pictures, screenshots, and photo albums into the presentation. The **Illustrations** group has commands to insert charts, smart graphics, and shapes. The **Add-ins** group allows you to insert apps and add-ins into a slide. You can add hyperlinks and actions to an object on a slide using the **Links** group. Add comments to a slide using the **Comments** group. The **Text** group helps you to insert text boxes, header & footer, Word art, date & time, slide number and objects. The **Media** group allows you to insert video or audio either from your PC or from online or a screen recording.

Design tab

This tab has commands to modify the slide theme, size, and background.

The **Themes** group allows you to apply themes to the Slides. In PowerPoint 2016, you can choose from thirty-two different themes.

The **Variants** group allows you to change the theme color, font, effects and background styles.
The **Customize** group allows you to change the slide size and format background.

You can click the scroll down arrow to display the next row of the theme in the **Themes** group. Use the up and down arrows to view the previous and next row of themes from the **Themes** group. click on the **More** drop down arrow button to display the entire **Theme** gallery on the **Themes** group.

You can point to various thumbnails in the Theme gallery to view live preview on the slide.

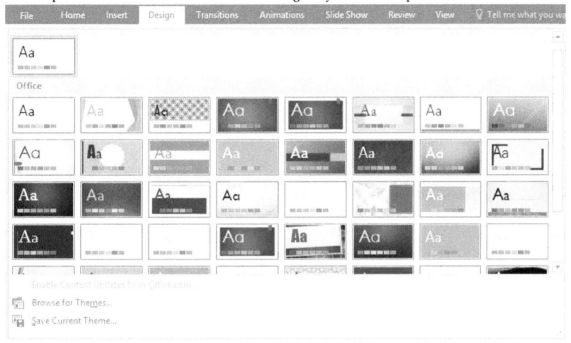

Transitions tab

The **Transitions** tab is used to add animation effects that happen between two or more slides.
On the **Transitions** tab, you can view commands related to the movement from slide to slide of your presentation. There are three groups of commands on this tab: **Preview**, **Transition to This Slide**, and **Timing**.

To view the transitions click on the **More drop down arrow** from the **Transition to this Slide** group on the **Transitions** tab. You can also click on the Up and Down arrow buttons to view the previous and next row of transitions. It displays the gallery of Transitions, which has three categories: *Subtle, Exciting, and Dynamic Content.*

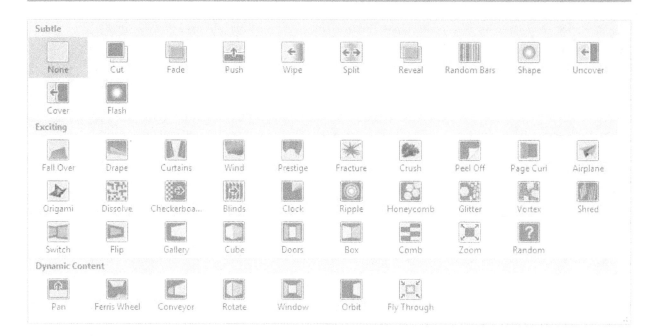

After applying a transition to the slide, you can preview it by clicking on the **Preview** button from the **Preview** group on the **Transitions** tab.

Animations tab

On the **Animations** tab, you can view the commands related to the animation of objects in four different groups: **Preview, Animation, Advanced Animation**, and **Timing**.

Note: Until you select an object on the slide, all buttons on the **Animations** tab are unavailable except **Preview, Animation Pane**, and **Reorder Animation**.

After selecting any object on the slide, the **Animation** effects are available on the ribbon.

To view the animation effects click on the Up and down arrow buttons (or) click on the **More** button to see the entire gallery of **Animation Effects** from the **Animation** group on the **Animation** tab.

The animation effects are of four types: *Entrance, Emphasis, Exit, and Motion Paths.*

Slide Show tab

This tab allows you to start, set up, record and monitor slide shows. The **Slide Show** tab displays commands in three different groups: *Start Slide Show, Set Up and Monitors.*

The **Start Slide Show** group allows you to begin the slide show either from the beginning or the current slide. It also has tools to present a slide online and create a custom slide. A custom slide is used to shorten the presentation by selecting only the required slides you want to use. The **Set Up** group allows you to specify the settings of a slide show, hide slide, rehearse timing and a record slide show. **Monitors** group enables you to use the presenter view if you are working on two monitors.

Review tab

This tab has commands to proofread, translate, add comments, compare, and sketch on the slide. The **Proofing** group allows you to proofread your presentation and Look for more words using Thesaurus. The **Insights** group enables you to search the selected text on the internet. The **Language** group allows you to translate the text into any other language by using online sources. You can set the language preference for proofing, editing, and text display. The **Comments** group allows you to add comments to the presentation. You can review the comments by using the **Show Comments** option. You can also delete comments using the **Delete** option. The **Compare** group allows you to compare the reviewed document with the original document. You can accept or reject the changes.

The **Ink** group allows you to add pen and highlighter stokes to your document. As you click on the **Start Inking** option, the **Ink Tools** tab appears on the ribbon.

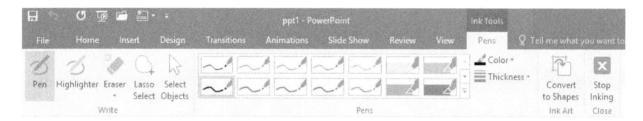

You can use different types of pens or highlighters to create strokes on the slide. To close the tab, click on the **Stop Inking** button from the **Close** group.

View tab

This tab has commands to zoom, fit or change the view mode. You can switch between different view modes by using the **Presentation Views** group. The **Master Views** group allows you to set the master pages of slides, handouts, and notes. The **Show** group enables you to show/hide rulers, grid, guides, and notes. The **Zoom** group has options to magnify the slide to various sizes, and fit the slide to the window size. You can also zoom in/out using the slider available on the Status bar on the lower right corner of the window. The **Color/Grayscale** group allows you to switch to color, grayscale or black and white. The **Window** group enables you to switch between windows of multiple files. The **Macros** group enables you to create and run macros.

Tell Me

In **Microsoft PowerPoint 2016**, you can see the **Tell me** box available on the ribbon. click in this box, type in a keyword, and press enter; a list of commands or options related to the keyword appear. The **Tell me** feature is one of the best features of Microsoft PowerPoint 2016; you can get help by just typing the keyword you want to try. For example, type 'online' in the **Tell me** box to view the search results, as shown.

Click in the **Tell me** box and notice a list. By default, the list shows start presentation, change the layout of the slide, change slide background, insert an image from the web, and add online video. You can either select an option from the list or enter a keyword in the **Tell me** box.

You can even get online help, by selecting **Get Help on "online"** from the list. Note that you need to connect to the internet to get the online help.

The Status Bar

The Status Bar is available below the Slides. It shows slide numbers and word count, and displays whether the document is free from proofing errors or not. You can add **Notes, Comments** and switch to different **Views** using the options on the status bar. You can zoom in/out by using the **Zoom Slider** (or) start a slide show using the Slide Show button.

Presentation Views

There are five different types of presentation views: Normal, Outline, Slide Sorter, Notes Page, and Reading.

Normal View: The Normal View is the default presentation view. In this view, the current slide appears along with slide thumbnails at the left side. You can add text, images, and other objects to the slide. The thumbnails available at the left-side allow you to navigate between the slides and rearrange them.

Outline View: In this view, the slide thumbnails are replaced with the outline pane. You can navigate between the slides using the outline pane.

Slide Sorter View: In this view, you can see all slides of your presentation at once. The main feature of this view is that you can rearrange the slides by clicking and dragging them.

Note Page View: In this view, a page displays a slide along with a speaker note. A speaker note contains elements other than text. You can edit the speaker note in this view. You can double-click on a slide, if you want to edit it.

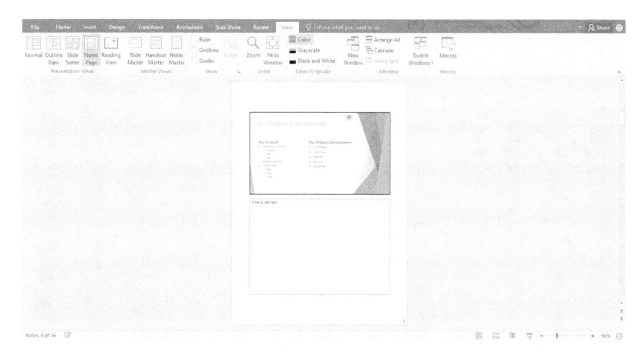

Reading View: In this view, you can play slide show in the PowerPoint window without switching to the full screen mode. You can also include animations and transitions in the slide show.

Saving a Presentation

After creating a presentation, you have to save the file. Saving a presentation is same as saving any other Microsoft Office program files like Word or Excel or Visio. However, you can also save your presentation when working on it. This saves the changes and avoids loss of the file. If you opened an existing presentation and made changes, then click the **Save** button on the **Quick Access Toolbar** to save the changes.

To save a presentation:
1. Click the **File** tab.

2. Click **Save** or **Save As**; PowerPoint displays a **Save As** page.
3. Click **Browse**; the **Save As** dialog box appears.
4. Select the Folder where you want to save on your computer.
5. Type a text in the **File name** box.
6. Click the **Save as Type** drop down arrow to change the file type. By default, the file type is PowerPoint Presentation.
7. Click **Save.**

Saving Files on OneDrive

You can save your presentation to OneDrive and share it with your colleagues if you are working in an organization. You need to log-in to your Microsoft Account to access the OneDrive. Saving files to OneDrive allows you to share files easily with other people and is a convenient way to back up essential files. You can give or deny permission to access your presentation on OneDrive. The storage location of OneDrive may be your company's Microsoft SharePoint environment or cloud-based storage location which is associated with your Microsoft Account.

To save files on OneDrive:
1. Click the **File** tab.
2. Click **Save As.**
3. Click **OneDrive.**
4. Click **Sign In** and sign into your Microsoft account.
5. Now, specify the OneDrive folder in which you want to save the file.
6. Click the **File name** text box.
7. Enter **File name.**
8. Click the **Save** button.

Closing a Presentation

After working with your presentation, you can close it. Closing a presentation gives you space to access other files on your computer. If you close an unsaved file, then PowerPoint asks you to save the presentation to avoid loss of your presentation.

To close the presentation:
1. Click the **Close** ✖ button on the top right corner of the window; it closes the presentation and exits PowerPoint window.
2. You can also click the **File** tab and select **Close** from the Backstage View; PowerPoint displays a message asking whether you want to save changes.
3. Click **Save** to save the changes.
   A. Click the **Don't Save** button, if you do not want to save the changes.
   B. Click the **Cancel** button, to stop closing the presentation.

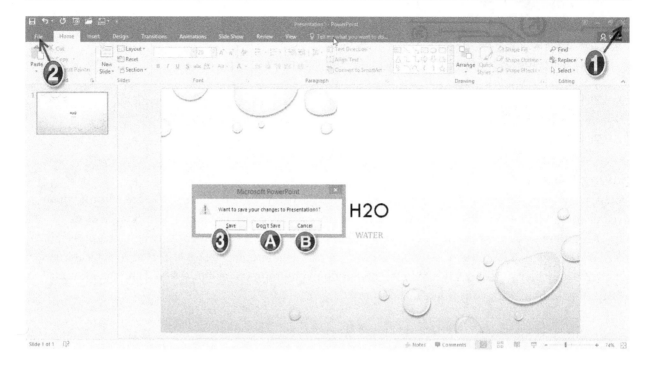

Keyboard Shortcut: Press Alt + F4 to close the presentation.

Deleting a Presentation

Sometimes, you may find some unnecessary files or out dated information which you no longer need. You can delete the unwanted presentation file from the **Open** dialog box. Deleting the unwanted or old files gives much space on your hard drive, so that you can work on other files on your PC. Before deleting the presentation make sure that the file is backed up, so that in future you may need it.

To delete a presentation:

1. Click the **File** tab.
2. Click **Open**.
3. Click **Browse**. It displays the **Open** dialog box.
4. Select the presentation that you want to delete (or) right-click on the file and select **Delete**; PowerPoint deletes the presentation and stores in the Recycle Bin.

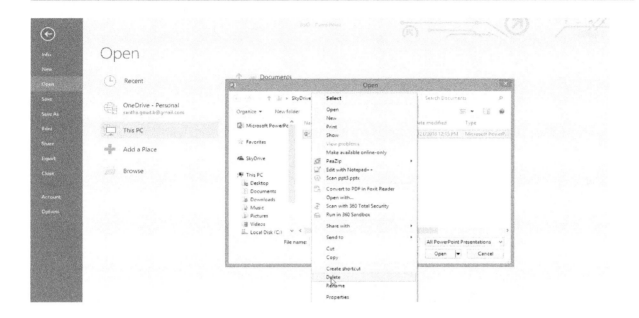

Chapter 2: Creating Presentations

In this chapter, you learn to

- Create a PowerPoint presentation
- Enter text in placeholders
- Edit & format text
- Create templates
- Apply themes
- Use the slide master
- Create headers and footers
- Use the Backstage view

In this chapter, you start by creating a presentation from scratch. Then you'll learn how to build a template, apply themes, modify slides and slide layouts in your presentation. Also, you learn to add headers and footers to slides.

Creating a Blank Presentation

To create a presentation, click the **PowerPoint 2016** on the Apps grid; the Backstage View appears showing different templates to create a presentation.

The **Blank Presentation** template is used to start a presentation from scratch. You need to have a good idea about the content and design of your presentation while using this template.

In the Backstage View, click the **Blank Presentation** template; a presentation appears with a blank slide. You can notice dotted borders on the slide. They are called Content Placeholders and you can add content to them. You can see dotted borders only while adding content to the slides. You cannot see them while running a slide show.

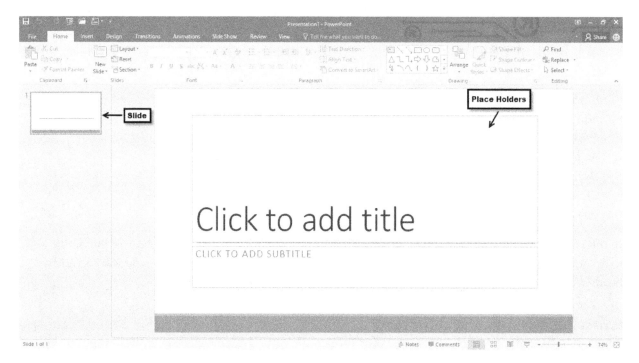

Entering Text in Placeholders

Entering text in Placeholders is very simple. You can do so using two different methods. These methods are discussed next.

Entering Text in the Normal View

Place the pointer in a text placeholder; it turns to I-beam pointer. click in the placeholder and notice that a blinking cursor appears, which indicates to enter the text. Enter text in placeholders; it appears on the slide and slide thumbnail pane. You can change the text format using the tools in the **Paragraph** group of the **Home** tab. In addition to text, you can insert other element type such as tables, pictures, videos, charts, and so on. You will learn about them in later chapters.

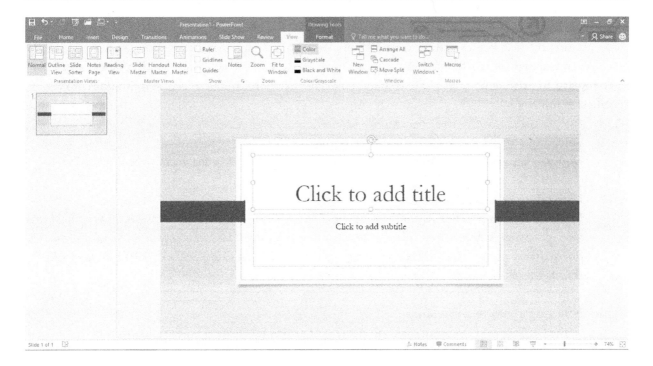

Entering Text in the Outline View

To enter text in the Outline view, click on the **View** tab > **Presentation Views** group > **Outline View**. Notice the outline pane at the left side of the window. click in the outline pane and enter the text; the entered text appears in the slide. You can also copy the text from any source and paste it in the outline pane. Note that you can insert only text in the outline pane. You cannot insert the objects such as images, graphics and shapes in the outline pane. Instead, you can add images or other graphics directly to the slide placeholders.

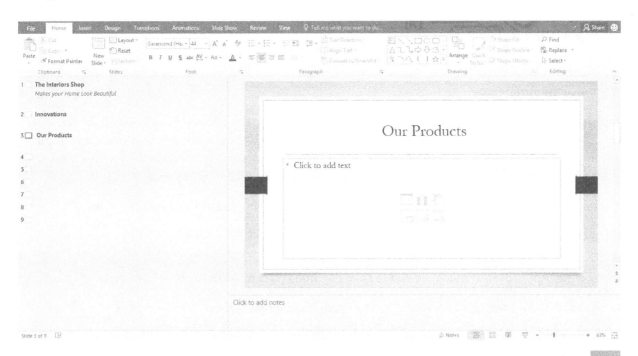

Editing Text

After entering the text, you can edit it as usual using word processing techniques. You can also enter a new text and change the existing text. To enter a new text, click where you want to add the text and enter it. To replace an existing text, select the text and enter the text. Some of the selecting techniques are specified as follows:

1. **Selecting a Word**
   Double-click anywhere in the word; this will automatically select the entire word.

2. **Using the Shift and arrow keys**
   Position the cursor at the beginning of the text you want to select and hold the Shift key and press the right arrow key to select adjacent word or line at a time. The same way you can also press the down arrow key to select the below paragraph at a time. Pressing Shift + Ctrl + Right arrow key selects the entire word.

3. **Selecting all the text of a slide**
   In the Outline view, you can select all the text of a slide by clicking on the slide icon in the Outline pane.

4. **Selecting all the text in a placeholder**
   Click in the placeholder of a slide and then click **Home** tab > **Editing** group > **Select** button > **Select All**. It selects the text of that particular placeholder only.

5. **Selecting all objects on a slide**
   Click on the border an object. Now click the **Home** tab > **Editing** group > **Select** button > **Select All.** All objects of the slide are selected. Now, you can work with all the objects as a unit.

6. **Selecting Bullet Points**
   Click on a bullet point and then click **Home** tab > **Editing** group > **Select** button > **Select All**; all the bullet point along with the sub points are selected. You can either click the bullets of the slide in the outline pane.

Tip: *The selected text is highlighted on the slide or in the outline pane. You can view the selection in the **Selection** pane. To open the **Selection** pane, click the **Home** tab > **Editing** group >Select button > **Selection Pane**. It will display all the selected objects. In this pane you can hide or show a particular object. click on the eye icon to hide an object. You can also hide all objects of the slide by clicking on the **Hide All** button in the selection pane.*

Keyboard Shortcuts: You can select all the text of a placeholder by clicking in it and Ctrl + A.

Cut, Copy and Paste the selected text

In PowerPoint 2016, you can reuse the text by using the Cut, Copy and Paste features same as in word. To avoid typing the same text manually and to save the time you can use these three features.

- **Cut** is used to copy the text and remove from its original location.
- **Copy** is used to duplicate the text and the original text remains in the same place.

- **Paste** is used to place the copied text (copied using either Cut or Copy) in another location.

Note: You also can cut, copy and paste objects like pictures, shapes, placeholders etc.

To Cut, Copy and Paste Text:

1. Click on the **Home** tab **> Dialog box launcher** button  in the **Clipboard** group; the **Clipboard** task pane appears on the left.
2. Select the text from the text placeholder of a slide using click and drag method or any select text methods.
3. Click the **Cut** button from the **Clipboard** group on the **Home** tab; it removes the selected text and places it on the **Windows Clipboard** which you can notice in the **Clipboard** task pane.
4. Select a text from the placeholder and click the **Copy** button from the **Clipboard** group on the **Home** tab; the selected text is duplicated appears in the Clipboard.
5. Select the slide where you want to paste the copied text.
6. Click the placeholder where you want to paste. You can notice that an insertion point appears.
7. In the **Clipboard** pane, select the copied text; it will be pasted at the cursor location. You can also click the **Paste** button on the **Clipboard** group to paste the most recently copied item.

TIP: You can also use keyboard shortcuts to cut, copy and paste the selected text or selected objects.

Keyboard Shortcuts:

Cut	Press Ctrl + X
Copy	Press Ctrl + C
Paste	Press Ctrl + V

Formatting Text

The font and font size plays a vital role in your presentation. A good font helps the audience to you're the ideas in your presentation without straining their eyes. So, choose the font and font size in such a way that it is easily readable by audience. There are four types of fonts: serif fonts, sans serif fonts, script fonts and decorative fonts.

Serif Fonts are fonts which have cross strokes at the letter ends.

Sans Serif Fonts are fonts which do not have cross strokes at the letter ends.

Script Fonts are fonts which looks like handwriting.

Decorative Fonts are fonts which are stylish and playful.

A good font type and color gives professional and appealing look to your presentation. You can format the font color to make your presentation more attractive and easy to read. You can use font colors along with the text styles like bold or italic or text shadow in your presentation to highlight certain words. You can specify a font using standard or custom colors.

Format Font and Size

To format the text font and size:

1. Click the placeholder and select the text which you want to format.
2. Click the **Home** tab > **Dialog box launcher** from the **Font** group; the **Font** dialog box appears with the **Font** tab selected.
3. Click the **Latin text font** drop down arrow to select the font type. You can also use the **Font type** drop-down available on the Fonts group of the ribbon to change the font type.
4. Specify the font size by clicking on the **Size** up and down arrows. You can also use the Font Size drop-down available on the **Fonts** group to change the font size.
5. Click the **OK** button to apply the changes.

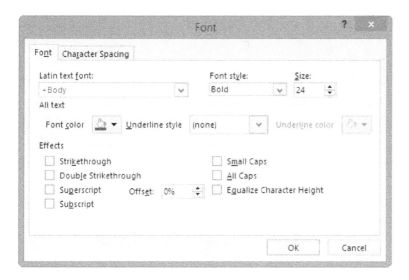

Format Font Color and Style

To format the font color and font style:

1. Click in the placeholder and select the text which you want to format.
2. Click the **Home** tab > **Font Color** drop down; it lists *Theme Colors, Standard Colors, More Colors,* and *Eyedropper* options.
3. Select the required color from the list.

You can also format the color using the **Font** dialog box.

4. In the **Font** dialog box, from the **All text** section, click the **Font color** drop down and select the required color from the list.
5. To select the font style, click the **Font style** drop down arrow. It lists four options: *Regular, Italic, Bold* and, *Bold Italic.*
6. To underline the selected text, then click on the **Underline Style** drop down.

It lists different styles of lines like, *Single Line, Double Line, Heavy Line, Dotted Line, Dashed Line, Wavy Line* and so on.

7. Select the appropriate underline style to apply. You can also apply the color to the underlined style.
8. To apply color to the underline, click on the **Underline Color** drop down from the **All text** section, and then select the required color from the list.
9. Click the **OK** button to apply changes.

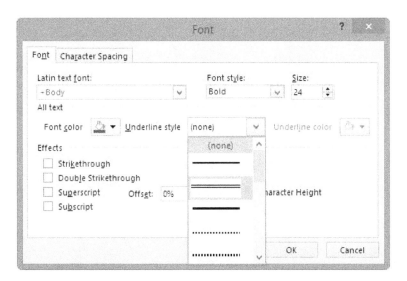

Add Effects to the text

To add effects to the text like *Superscript, Subscript, Strikethrough, Small Caps, All Caps* etc. then,

1. Click the placeholder and select the text to format.
2. Click the **Home** tab > **Font** group > **Dialog box launcher** ; it opens the **Font** dialog box with **Font** tab selected.
3. Select the required effect to apply by selecting the checkboxes in the **Effects** section.
4. Click the **OK** button to apply.

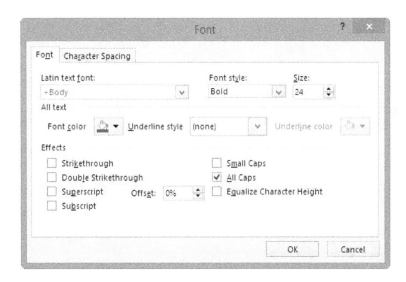

Templates and Themes

Microsoft PowerPoint offers various templates to create presentations. A template is a predesigned document that you can use to create slides easily without having to think about formatting. It is a collection of predesigned styles and formatting settings, which saves a lot of time. A template will be useful if you are representing an organization, which has brand image by its logo, color scheme, or other visual effects. You can impart the branding of your organization into the presentation by creating a template. Also, templates are very useful to give a unique look to your presentation.

There are two types of predesigned templates available in the PowerPoint: Design Templates and Content Templates.

Design Template: A design template is a blank presentation with a theme and graphics that are already applied to it.

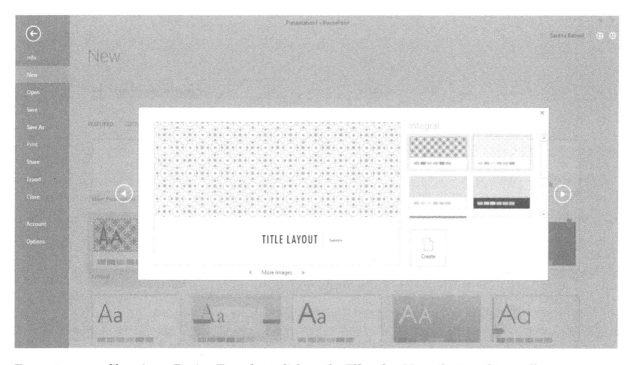

To create a new file using a Design Template, click on the **File** tab **> New**; the templates gallery appears on the Backstage View. You can notice a variety of design and content templates in the gallery. Select a template from the gallery; different color variations of the selected template appear. Select the required color variation and click the **Create** button; a new presentation is created using the selected template.

Content Template: A content template has some text along with predesigned graphics and colors. You can use these type of templates for specific purposes such as creating student certificates, awards, calendars, and so on. You can search for a specific type of content template in the **Search** box, if you are online. For example, enter certificates in the **Search** box; a number of certificate templates appear in the gallery. Select a template from the gallery, and then click the **Create** button. Now, edit the text in the presentation based on your requirement. For example, if you have created a presentation using the

Employee of the Year certificate template, then you need to change the Name of the company and employee.

Note: You can search the templates and themes in the search box only if connected to the internet.

Changing Themes

PowerPoint provides you with various predefined color settings called themes. You can apply themes to give a unique look to the presentation.

To change theme:
1. Click the **Design** tab on the ribbon.
2. Click the down arrow at the bottom right corner of the **Themes** group; the Theme gallery appears. On the **Themes** gallery place the cursor on the theme to view its preview.
3. Select a suitable theme from the **Themes** gallery; it will be applied to the entire presentation; You can also apply a separate theme to each slide.
4. Select the slide from the left-side pane.
5. Right click on the theme in the **Themes** gallery.
6. Select **Apply to Selected Slides**.

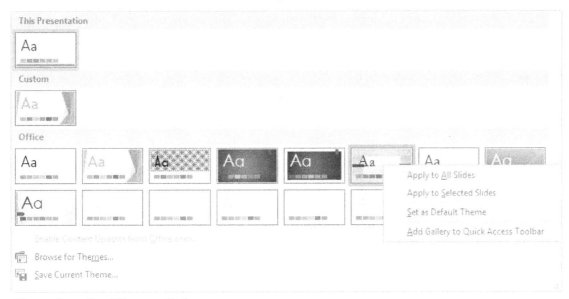

Changing the Theme Colors

You can change the color of the selected theme by selecting a color variant from the **Variants** group. To access more color variants, click the down arrow at the bottom right corner of the **Variants** group, and then select a color from the **Colors** drop-down.

You can create a new theme color by clicking on the **Customize Colors** option from the **Colors** drop down list; the **Customize Theme Colors** dialog appears. On this dialog, change the colors for text backgrounds, accents, and hyperlinks from the drop-downs available next to each option. Type-in the color variant name in the **Name** box and click **Save**.

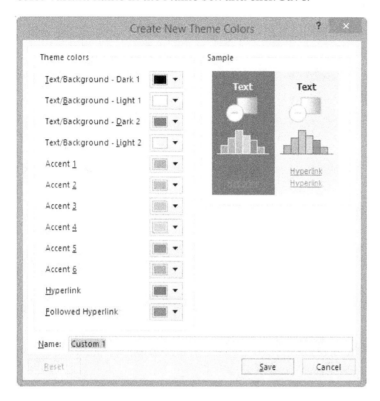

Likewise, you can change the Fonts, Effects, and Background Styles from the **Variants** gallery.

Headers and Footers

Footer is a small workup text that appears at the bottom of every slide. You can easily add a footer to include thing like the copy right the word confidential at the bottom of all your slides.

If you're printing handouts you can also add a header such as the presentation title which will be printed out with every slide.

To add a Header:

1. Click on the **Insert** tab.

2. Click **Header and Footer** on the **Text** group on the ribbon; the **Header and Footer** dialog box opens with two tabs **Slide** and **Notes and Handouts**.

3. Click the **Notes and Handouts** tab.

4. Select the **Header** option.

5. Type in the text like title name, company name, and so on; it will appear on the upper left corner of the Handouts.

6.   Click the **Apply to All** button.

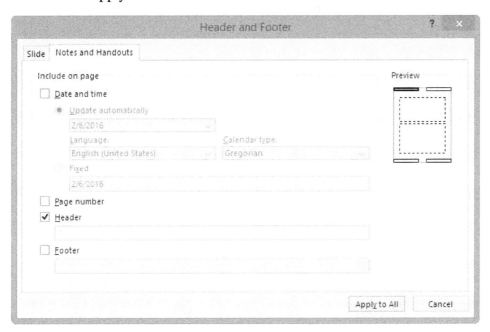

Note: The Headers text appears only on the printed handouts. You can view the header text on the handouts at the upper left corner.

To add a **Footer**:

1.   Click the **Slide** tab in the **Header and Footer** dialog box.
2.   Select the **Footer** option.
3.   Enter the text; It will appear at the lower middle of the slide.
4.   Click the **Apply** button. click **Apply to All** to add the footer to all the presentation slides.

Adding Date to Slides

You can add a date to the slides as per your computers system date. You can add date in slide master view instead adding date to the individual slides. Adding date in slide master view saves lot of time. To add date in slide master view, click **View** tab > **Master Views** group > **Slide Master** on the ribbon. Select the Master slide from the Thumbnails pane. On the **Slide Master** tab of the ribbon, click the **Master Layout** from the **Master Layout** group; the **Master Layout** dialog box appears. Select the **Date** option and click **OK**. The date appears on all slides. Note that the date appears only on particular layout if you select that layout from the Thumbnails pane enable the **Date** option. click **Close Master View** on the ribbon to switch to the normal view.

To add a date to slides in the normal view:

1. Click on the **Insert** tab.
2. Click **Header and Footer** on the **Text** group on the ribbon. The **Header and Footer** dialog box opens with two tabs **Slide, Notes and Handouts**.
3. Select the **Date and Time** option.
4. Select the **Update automatically** radio button to update the date and time automatically as per the US calendar.
5. Select the date format from the drop-down available below the **Update automatically** option.

If you select the **Fixed** radio button, the date of creation will appear on the presentation.

6. Click the **Apply** button.

Note: The date appears at the lower left corner of the slide. If you click the **Apply to All** button, the date appears on all slides of your presentation.

Adding Slide Numbers

You can number the presentation slides automatically and position it anywhere on the footer of the slide. In Slide Master view, you can add slide numbers by clicking on the **Slide Master** tab. Select the **Master Slide** and click on the **Master Layout**; the **Master Layout** dialog box appears. Select the **Slide Number** option and click **OK**. The slide numbers appear on all slides. The date appears on all slides. Note that the slide number appears only on particular layout if you select that layout from the Thumbnails pane enable the **Slide Number** option

To add slide numbers in normal view:

1. Click the **Insert** tab.
7. Click **Header and Footer** on the **Text** group on the ribbon. The **Header and Footer** dialog box opens with two tabs **Slide, Notes and Handouts**.
2. Select the **Slide number** option.
3. Select the **Don't show on title slide** option; The slide number, date & time, footer notes will not appear on the title slide.
4. Click on the **Apply** button.

Note: The slide number will appear at the lower right corner of the slide. If you click the **Apply to All** button, the slide numbers will appear on all slides except title slide (if **Don't show on title slide** is selected).

Working with Backstage

You can manage PowerPoint presentation commands like creating, opening, saving, printing, sharing files, and so on from the backstage view. If you have opened the presentation, then click on the **File** tab to display the **Backstage view**. The backstage view will display the basic info about the presentation like how many slides, template, size, title, created on, last modified and so on in the **Info page**.

To open another PowerPoint file then click on the **Open** option and **Browse** the file. The present file will be still opened after opening another file. You can also save the file using save and save as options, you can print the slides, you can even share the file from the backstage view. To go back to file, click on the **Arrow Button** at the top left corner of the page.

You can even manage the PowerPoint options by clicking on the **Options** button, which will be discussed later in the next chapters.

Presentation1 - PowerPoint

Info

Protect Presentation

Control what types of changes people can make to this presentation.

Protect
Presentation ˅

Inspect Presentation

Before publishing this file, be aware that it contains:
- Document properties and author's name
- Content that people with disabilities are unable to read

Check for
Issues ˅

Manage Presentation

Check in, check out, and recover unsaved changes.
- There are no unsaved changes.

Manage
Presentation ˅

Properties ˅

Size	Not saved yet
Slides	1
Hidden slides	0
Title	Add a title
Tags	Add a tag
Categories	Add a category

Related Dates

Last Modified
Created   Today, 2:58 PM
Last Printed

Related People

Author

                 Add an author
Last Modified By Not saved yet

Show All Properties

Chapter 3: Working with Slides

In this chapter, you will learn to:

- Add and remove Slides
- Navigate through Slides
- Create custom layouts
- Divide slides into sections
- Rearrange slides
- Duplicate slides
- Copy & paste slides
- Hide a slide

In the last chapter, you have learned to add slides to a presentation. Now, you will learn to perform some basic operations such as removing, navigating, rearranging, and dividing slides. Also, you will learn to create custom slides.

Adding and Removing Slides

You can add a new slide with the desired layout using the **New Slide** drop-down on the **Slide** group of the **Home** tab. There are different number of slide layouts like *Title and Content, Section Header, Two Content, Comparison, Title Only, Blank, Content with Caption, Picture with Caption, Title and Caption, Quote with Caption, Name Card, Quote Name Card and True or False*. The slide layouts are based on the template of your presentation, it may list some additional slide layouts based on the template you choose.

Depending on the slide layout the placeholder may vary. For example, if you select a Blank layout, it does not have any placeholder. By default, each added slide has the layout of the preceding slide.

You can add a slide by following anyone of the methods:

1. Click on the **Home** tab > **Slide** group > **New Slide** button,
2. Press **Ctrl + M** keyboard shortcut.
3. Right-click the slide in the **Thumbnails pane** in **Normal View** and select **New Slide**; a new a slide is added after the title slide. The new slide has the same layout as the preceding slide.

To add a new slide with different layout:

1. Click on the **Home** tab > **Slides** group **> New Slide** drop down; it displays a gallery of slide layouts.
2. Select the required layout from the gallery; the elements of the layout are based on the template of your presentation.

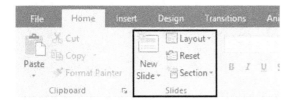

Note: You can also right-click the slide in the **Thumbnails pane** in **Normal View** and click on **Layout** option; It expands with different slide layouts based on the template of your presentation.

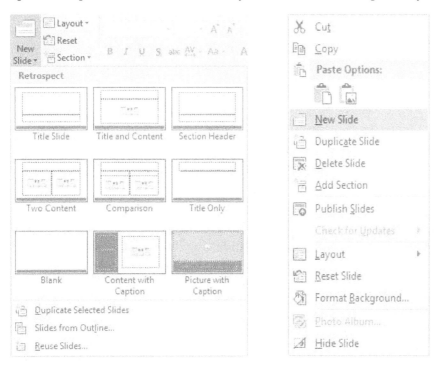

Changing the Slide Layout

You can change the layout from the **Layout Gallery**.

To change the slide layout:

1. Select the slide that you want to change.
2. Click on the **Home** tab > **Layout** drop down; it displays a gallery of slide layouts.
3. Select the desired layout from the gallery.

PowerPoint changes the slide layout to the selected layout.

Removing Slides

In some cases, you may want to remove a slide or slides from a presentation. If some slides of a presentation are obsolete, then you may want to remove them. PowerPoint provides various ways to remove slides.

There are three methods to remove a slide. You can delete it either in the **Thumbnails pane** in **Normal View** or in the **Slide Sorter View** or in the **Outline pane** in the **Outline View**.

To remove a slide in the **Normal View**:

1. Select the slide to delete from **Thumbnails Pane** and press the **Delete** key on the Keyboard. (or)
2. Right click on the selected slide, and then select the **Delete Slide** option.

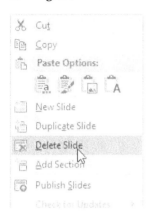

Note: If you want to delete more than one slide, then select the **first slide** and hold down the **Shift** key and select the **last slide**. Press thee **Delete** key on the Keyboard to delete them. If the slides are not in the order to delete, then select the first slide and hold down the **Ctrl** key while selecting other slide.

To remove a slide in the Slide Sorter view:

1. Click on the **View** tab > **Presentation Views** group > **Slide Sorter**.
2. Select the slide which you want to delete.
3. Right-click on the selected slide.
4. Select **Delete Slide** from the menu.

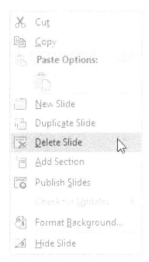

Likewise, you can delete a slide in any other view using the **Delete Slide** option.

Navigating Through Slides

Navigating between slides is very important to create a presentation. There are several different ways to navigate through slide. Some of them are discussed next.

- Clicking on the slides in the Thumbnails Pane.
- Using the **Previous Slide** and **Next Slide** buttons at the bottom of the scroll bar on the right hand side.

- Using the scroll bar on the right side.
- Press up and down arrow keys on the Keyboard.

Organizing Slides into Sections

When you are creating a presentation with more slides, you can divide them into sections. Sections are used to organize slide logically and professionally. They are not visible to the audience.

You can create sections in two different ways:

- Right click on the slide layout in the thumbnails pane and select **Add section**.
- Click the **Section** drop down and select **Add section** from the **Slides** group of the **Home** tab.

Sections will appear only in the **Normal View** and **Slide Sorter View**. They are not available in other views. Sections will not disturb the presentation nor will they create a new slide. They are used only to make the slides organized and format the presentation to give a professional look.

After creating sections, you can rename a section in two different ways:

- Right click the untitled section in the thumbnails pane and select **Rename section**.

- Select a section from the Thumbnails pane. click **Home** tab > **Slides** group > **Section** drop down > **Rename Section**; the **Rename Section** dialog box appears. Type the section name and click the **Rename** button.

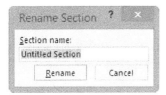

You can collapse or expand all sections by selecting the **Collapse All** option or **Expand All** option from the **Section** drop down on the **Home** tab.

You can also collapse or expand an individual section. To collapse section, click on the **Collapse Arrow** of the section. click on the **Expand Arrow** of the section to expand a section.

Hiding slides under section titles makes it easy to focus on some particular section of the presentation. This enables you to deliver a presentation with a consistent look and highlight specific portions. The intended audience are more likely receive the message with the help of sections.

Rearranging Slides

After you have added several slides to a presentation, sometimes you may want to rearrange the order of slides in a presentation, so that you efficiently communicate the message to the audience.

To rearrange the order of your slides, click on the **View** tab > **Presentation Views** group > **Slide Sorter View**. This view displays all slides at a time. Rearrange the slides and sections by dragging them.

You can also rearrange slides in the **Normal view**. For this, click the **View** tab > **Presentation Views** group > **Normal View**. In the **Thumbnails pane**, drag the slides up or down and arrange them in the desired order. Similarly, you can move sections up or down to rearrange them.

You can even copy slides from one presentation to another in the **Slide Sorter View** or **Normal View**. First, open both the presentations in **Slide Sorter View** or **Normal View**. click **View** tab > **Windows** group > **Arrange All** button. Now, drag the slides which you want to copy from one presentation window to the other presentation window.

Duplicating a Slide

In some cases, you may need to design a slide that is similar to the first one. You can use the **Duplicate Slide** option to copy the slide, and change it as your requirement. You can modify the duplicated slide by making some small changes to it. Creating another slide which is similar to the first one saves a lot of time.

To duplicate a slide:

1. Select the slide or slides that you want to duplicate in **Slide Sorter View**.
2. Click **Home** tab > **Slides** group > **New Slide** drop down.
3. Select the **Duplicate Selected Slides** option.

(or)

Right click the selected slide in the **Thumbnails pane** and select **Duplicate Slide**. Now, the selected slide or slides are duplicated.

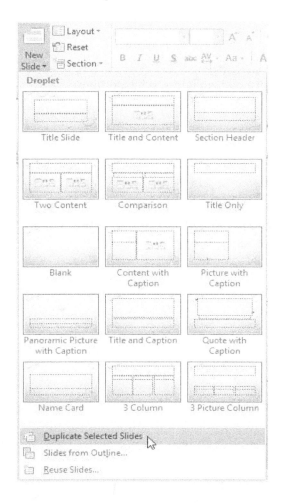

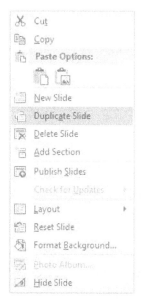

Note: If you want to select multiple slides, then click on the first slide, press & hold the **Ctrl** key and select other slides.

Copy and Paste a Slide

You can copy a slide or slides from one presentation and paste it into the other presentation. This saves a lot of time in creating other presentation. clicking and dragging the slides is another way to copy & paste them.

To copy and paste a slide:

1. Select the slide or slides that you want to copy in the **Slide Sorter View** or **Normal View**.
2. Click the **Home** tab > **Clipboard** group > **Copy** button.
3. Switch to the other presentation.
4. Click on the **Paste** drop down.
5. Select **Keep Source Formatting**.

PowerPoint pastes the slides that you have copied from the previous presentation.

Hiding a Slide

In some cases, you may need to prepare two presentations for two different audiences. For example, you may need to give a detailed presentation to your directors and a shortened one to executives. You can hide the slides that you do not want to show to your executives. This saves a lot of time as you are not required two separate presentations.

To hide a slide:

1. Select the slide or slides that you want to hide in the **Slide Sorter View** or **Normal View**.
2. Click the **Slide Show** tab.
3. Click the **Hide Slide** button on the **Set Up** group.

You can notice a diagonal line appears through the slide number in the **Slide Sorter View or Normal View**. This indicates that the slide will not be displayed during the slide show.

To unhide the hidden slides, select the hidden slide and click the Hide Slide button.

TIP: You can also hide a slide by selecting the slide in the **Thumbnails Pane** in the Normal View, right-clicking it, and selecting **Hide Slide** from the menu. This also works in **Slide Sorter View**. Right-click the selected slide and select **Hide Slide**.

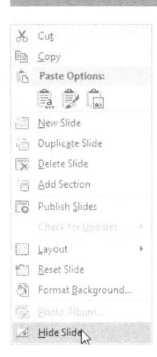

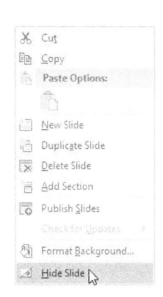

Chapter 4: Working with Master Views

Master Views

The appearance of a slide or page of a presentation is determined by the Master view. By default, each PowerPoint presentation has three Master views: Slide Master, Handout Master and Notes Master.

Slide Master: As the name indicates, it controls the appearance of the slides in your presentation. All the attributes such as theme, colors, fonts, background, effects, and so on are determined by the Slide Master. For example, if you want to insert a logo on all the slide layouts, simply open the slide master, and then insert a logo on it; the logo will be visible on all the slides.

Handout Master: It controls the appearance of the printed version of your presentation.

Notes Master: It determines the look of the printed notes.

Working with the Slide Master

To understand the slide master, you need to open it and view its various elements. To do so, click **View** tab > **Master Views** group > **Slide Master** . Notice the various elements of the Slide Master view, as shown.

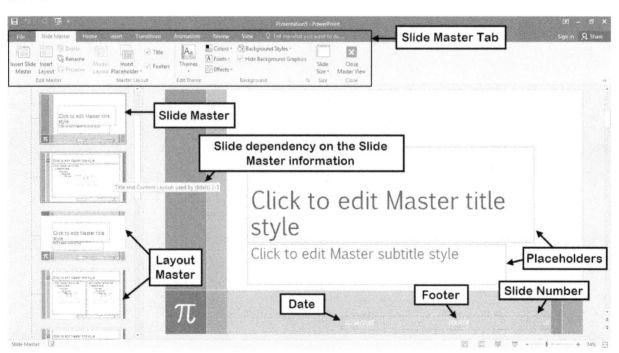

Various features of the Slide Master view are explained next:

Slide Master tab: The **Slide Master** tab appears on the ribbon, when you are in the Slide Master view. It has the tools to change the background, theme, size, and layout of the master slide. You can also insert or delete a slide master.

Slide Master: The Slide Master appears at the top in the Thumbnails pane and it is connected to all the layout masters. Place the cursor on the Slide Master and notice a message on it. It shows that all the layout masters are dependent on the Slide Master.

Layout Master: Earlier, you have learnt to create a new slide using different types of the slide layouts such as Title and Content, Two Content, Comparison, and so on. There is a separate layout master for each slide layout and they are displayed below the Slide master. If you want to make changes to a particular slide layout, then just modify the corresponding layout master.

Placeholders: The placeholders are used to enter text and other content. You can specify the text settings in the placeholders such as font, formatting, and so on. The specified settings will reflect in the slides.

Date, Footer, and Slide Number: These three placeholders are located at the bottom. You can change their location by selecting them and dragging or using the arrow keys.

You can notice that the **Design** and **Slide Show** tabs are unavailable when you open the **Slide Master** tab.

When you are finished modifying then click the **Close Master View** button on the ribbon.

Note: Any changes that you made to the presentation in the normal view will be retained after closing the slide master view. click the **Reset** button on the **Slides** group of the **Home** tab to apply the changes made in the slide master view.

Customizing Bulleted Lists in Slide Master

To customize the bullets in slide master view do as follows:

1. Activate the Slide Master View by clicking the **Slide Master View** button on the **View** ribbon tab.
2. Select the text at individual levels from the slide layout.
3. Click the **Home** tab > **Paragraph** group > **Bullets** drop down and select **Bullets and Numbering** option; the **Bullets and Numbering** dialog appears with **Bulleted** tab selected.
4. Click the **Customize** button at bottom right corner; the **Symbol** dialog box appears. On this dialog, you can the type of bullets from **Subset** drop down.
5. Select the appropriate symbol. You can see the **Unicode name** of that particular symbol at the bottom left.

6. Click the **OK** button to apply.
7. Again click the **OK** button to close the **Bullets and Numbering** dialog box.

TIP: You can also change the size and color of the bullet point. Also, you can add pictures by clicking on **Picture** button in the **Bullets and Numbering** dialog box. On doing so, the **Insert Picture** dialog box appears on the screen. Select the appropriate picture for bullets and click the **Open** button. Again, click the **OK** button to apply.

Editing Text Elements in Slide Master

You can use the tools available in the **Font** group to edit the text elements for all slide layouts in the slide master view.

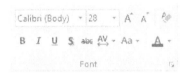

Font: Use this drop-down to change the font type.

Font Size: Use this drop-down to change the font size. You can use the **Increase Font Size** or **Decrease Font Size** option to change the font size.

1. Select the text from the placeholder of the **Slide Master** or select the text placeholder of the **Slide Master**.
2. Click **Home** tab > **Font** group and change the font type, font size, font color as required.
3. You can make the text bold, italic, underlined and apply text shadow as required.

Note: If you have selected the title text in the slide master, then the titles of all other slide layout are changed.

Modifying the Placeholders

To modify the placeholders in slide master view:

1. Select the placeholder that you want to modify; notice that the dotted border is replaced with solid border. The solid borders have the resize and rotate handle. The rotate handle appears at the top middle of the solid border.
2. Click and drag the resize handles to change the size of the placeholder.
3. Select the placeholder and drag it (while the mouse pointer turns to four arrow pointer) and place it anywhere on the slide; the position of the placeholder changes.
4. Click the rotate handle and rotate the placeholder as required.

Inserting a new Placeholders

To insert a new placeholder on the individual slide layout, click **Insert Placeholder** on the **Master Layout** group of the **Slide Master** tab; different types of placeholders appear. Select the appropriate placeholder type from the drop-down, drag it, and place it on the slide.

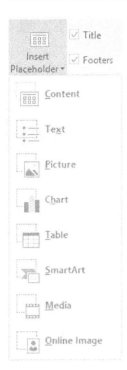

Inserting Logo or image

You can insert an image or logo to your presentation in the Slide Master View. To insert an image or logo click the Slide Master in the Thumbnails Pane. Now, click the **Insert** tab > **Images** group > **Pictures**; the **Insert Picture** dialog appears. Now, select the image from the folder and click the **Insert** button. You can click and drag the image to resize or position it anywhere on the slide.

Now, you can notice that image or logo on all the slides. Note that the image or logo may or not appear on all slide layouts depending on the theme of the slide. For example, if the title slide has a different design from other slide layouts, then you may need to insert the logo separately.

After inserting the image, you can format it by using **Format > Picture Tools** tab. You can apply styles, effects, borders, background, and adjust the brightness and color of the image from this tab.

Formatting Background in Slide Master View

You can change the background in the **Normal view** on the **Design** tab. However, it is easier to make changes to background from the **Slide Master** tab.

To format background for all slides:

1. Select the **Slide Master** from the thumbnail pane in the **Slide Master** view.

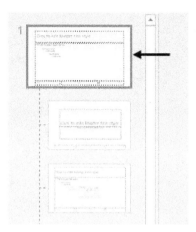

2. On the **Background** group, click **Background Styles > Format Background** option. You can also
    click the **Dialog box launcher** button of the **Background** group.
    It opens the **Format Background** pane on the right hand side.

By using the **Format Background** pane, you can set the background color, texture, pattern, or background
picture to all slides or the current slide.

You can also hide the background graphics in the slide master view. To hide the any graphics on the slide that are part of the theme, select the **Hide Background Graphics** checkbox from the **Background** group on the **Slide Master** tab (or) on the Fill page of the **Format Background** pane.

3. Select the *Solid Fill or Gradient Fill or Picture or Texture Fill or Pattern Fill* option from the Format Background pane. You can also select these background styles from the **Background Styles** drop-down.
4. Click the **Apply to All** button.

To format background for a particular slide:

1. Select the **Slide Layout** that you want to format in the **Slide Master** view.
2. On the **Background** group, click **Background Styles > Format Background** option.
3. Select the type of **Background Fill** from the **Format Background** pane. The selected background is applied the slide.
4. Click the **Close** on the **Format Background** pane.

Note: If you click the **Apply to All** button, then it will format all slides backgrounds including the slide master. To undo the formatting click the **Reset Background** button. The **Reset Background** button will be unavailable for the **Slide master**; you cannot reset the slide background in the **Slide master**. This option is available for individual slide layouts only.

Inserting a new Slide Master

In the slide master view, you can insert a new slide master by clicking on the **Insert Slide Master** from the **Edit Master** group.

By default, it applies **Office theme** to a new set of **Slide master**. You can change the theme of the slide master. To do so, select the slide master and click **Slide Master** tab > **Edit Theme** > **Themes** drop-down and select the theme from the theme gallery.

There is an another way to add a set of Slide Master. To do so, click **Slide Master** tab > **Edit Theme** > **Themes** drop-down, right-click on a theme in the theme gallery, and select **Add as New Slide Master**.

If you wish to use the same Theme for the entire presentation, but change the color variation then you can do it by duplicating the slide master and editing it. To do this, right click the **Slide Master** and select **Duplicate Slide Master**. Next, edit the theme color from the **Theme Colors** drop-down on the **Background** group. To identify the new slide master with a separated name, right click the it and select **Rename Master**. Type a new name in the **Rename Layout** dialog and click **Rename**.

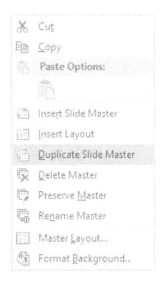

Preserve Master Slides

In PowerPoint 2016, a set of Master Slides is preserved so that you can use it in future. When a set of Master Slides is preserved, PowerPoint will avoid deleting it from the presentation, if it is not in use.

However, you can also delete a set of Master Slides in Slide Master view even it is a preserved Master Slide.

By default, a Master slide is preserved. However, you can preserve a set of Master Slides, if it is not preserved.

1. Click the **Slide Master** tab.
2. Select the set of Slide Master you want to preserve.

Note: Make sure you select the Slide Master and not the slide layout.

3. Click **Preserve** from the **Edit Master** group.

TIP: The **Preserve** button is available only if there is more than one set of Slide Master. Otherwise, it is unavailable (grayed out).

You can view a **Preserve** icon appears on the thumbnails pane of slide master. You can also, click the preserve icon on the thumbnails pane.

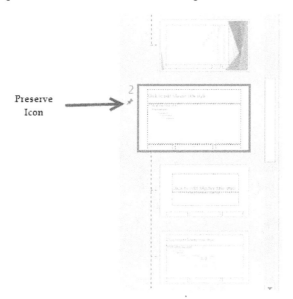

To unpreserved the set of Master slides, then repeat the steps 1 to 3 again. You can notice, the preserve icon disappears if you unpreserved it.

Changing Slide Layouts

To change the slide layout, go to **Home** tab > **Slides** group > **Layout** drop down and select the desired layout from the gallery. You can also right click the slide and select **Layout** option, it expands and opens the **Layout Gallery**. You can select the desired layout.

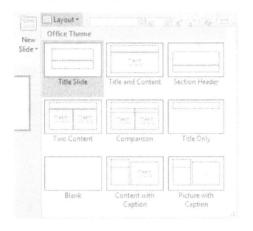 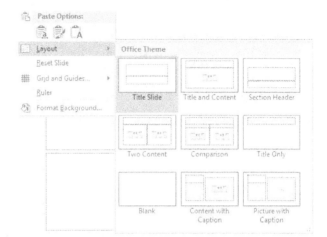

You can also create your own layouts in PowerPoint 2016. To insert a new layout, click the **View** tab > **Slide Master**; it opens **Slide Master** tab. On the **Slide Master** tab, click **Insert Layout** in the **Edit Master** group. It creates a new layout with a title but no other contents. You can format it by inserting placeholders and arranging them as required.

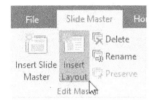

Placeholders are used to hold specific type of content like *text, pictures, tables, charts, media, SmartArt*, etc. to the slide layouts.

To insert a text placeholder, click the **Insert Placeholders** drop down and select the **Text**. Specify the first and second corners of the placeholder. You can click and drag the placeholder to specify its position. After inserting the placeholder, you can format the content by increasing the font size, and applying bold, color, and bullets. You can insert multiple placeholders such as Picture, Chart, and so on in the same slide.

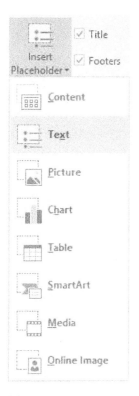

After inserting placeholders, name the layout by right clicking the Custom Layout and select **Rename Layout**.

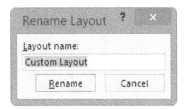

Give it a name and click the **Rename** button and close the slide master by clicking the **Close Master View** button. Now, you can use this layout wherever you need. It saves time and effort.

Changing Themes, Theme Colors, Theme Fonts and Theme Effects

In the slide master view, you can change the themes, theme color, fonts and effects. If none of the themes, theme colors, theme fonts match your requirement, then you can create your own theme, theme color and theme font. However, the default themes provided in PowerPoint are selected based on good design principles and look professional.

To change the theme:

1. Click the **Slide Master** tab > **Edit Theme** group > **Themes**; it displays a gallery of themes with forty-one different types of themes and three commands.
2. Click the **Browse for Themes** option to browse for more themes; it opens the **Choose Theme or Themed Document** dialog box.
3. Select the required theme from the folder.
4. Click the **Open** button.

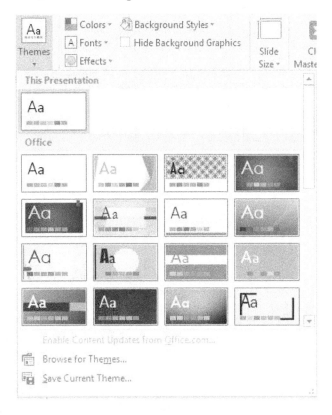

To save the theme:

1. On the ribbon, click the **Slide Master** tab > **Edit Theme** group > **Themes** gallery.
2. Select the **Save Current Theme** option from the gallery; the **Save Current Theme** dialog box appears.
3. Enter the **File name**.
4. Click the **Save** button.

TIP: You can set any theme or custom theme as a default theme. To do so, click the **Design** tab > **Themes** group > **More** drop down and select any theme from the gallery. Right-click and select **Set as Default Theme**.

The same way, you can change the theme color. To change the theme color:

1. Click the **Slide Master** tab > **Background** group > **Colors**. The **Colors** gallery with twenty-three sets of theme colors and two commands appears.
2. Select the required theme color from the gallery.

In the **Colors** gallery, the individual set of theme colors are represented by 8 of its 12 colors.

You can see a live preview on the selected slide by placing the cursor on the set of theme colors in the gallery.

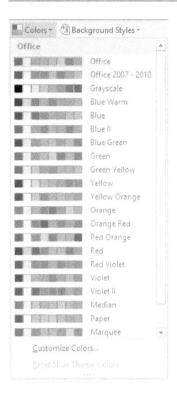

You can also create a new theme color. To create a custom theme color:

1. Select the **Customize Colors** option from the **Colors** drop-down; it opens the **Create New Theme Colors** dialog box.

   In this dialog box, there are 12 type of theme colors. These colors are explained next:

   - **Text/Background:** There four types of Text/Background colors. The dark text color is used for light background or vice-versa.
   - **Accent 1 to Accent 6:** There are six type accent colors that are used for other objects except text.
   - **Hyperlink:** This color is used for hyperlinks.
   - **Followed Hyperlink:** It is used to indicate the already visited hyperlink.

2. Change the Text/Background, Accent, Hyperlink and Followed Hyperlink colors as required. You can preview the change in the Sample section.
3. Click the **Reset** button on the bottom left of the dialog box, if you want to reset the colors.
4. Enter the name of custom theme color in the **Name** box.
5. Click the **Save** button to save the changes (or) click the **Cancel** button, to discard the changes.

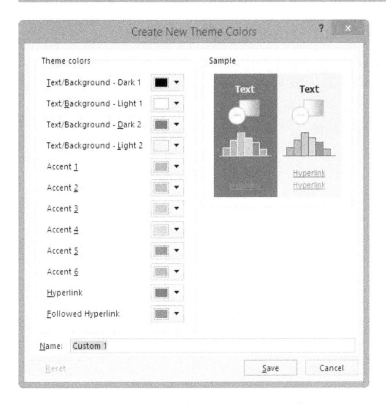

To view the custom theme color (that you created):

1. Click the **Slide Master** tab > **Background** group.
2. Click the **Colors** drop down; the custom theme color appears under **Custom** section.

Note: You can also view the custom theme color by clicking on the **Design** tab > **Variants** group > **More drop down** and select the **Colors** option. It expands a gallery of theme colors and the custom theme color that you have created.

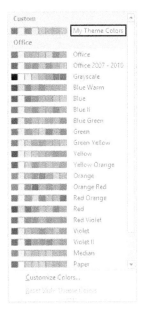

To change the theme fonts in the Slide Master view:

1. Click the **Slide Master** tab > **Backgrounds** group > **Fonts**; it lists a gallery with 25 different fonts and one command. The individual set of theme fonts contains two fonts or two variations of the same font.

2. Select the **Customize Fonts** option from the list; it opens the **Create New Theme Font** dialog box.
3. Click the **Heading Font** drop down and select the heading font.
4. Click the **Body Font** drop down and select the body font; you can see the preview in the **Sample** section, as you change the Fonts.

    Note: Heading Font is used for the slide titles and the Body Font is used for other text in the slide.

5. Enter the name of the theme font in the **Name** box.
6. Click the **Save** button to save the theme fonts (or) click the **Cancel** button or **Close** button on the top right of the dialog box to discard the changes.

TIP: You can also change the theme, theme color, theme font and theme effects and background from the **Design** tab. To do so, click the **Design** tab > **Variants** group > **More** drop down and select the appropriate one (Colors or Fonts or Effects or Background Styles).

Preparing the Speaker Notes

Speaker Notes help you to deliver a presentation to your audience, very smoothly. Each slide of a presentation has a notes pane at the bottom of the slide, in the Normal View. You can create notes related to the topic of the slide by opening the Notes Page view. To do so, click **View > Presentation Views > Notes Pages**. In the **Notes Pages**, the notes placeholder appears below the slide. In the notes area, you can type text and include graphics or shapes or images. You can also print the notes to rehearse the presentation before delivering it.

You can add Speaker Notes to all slides in your presentation.

To add Speaker Notes, click the **Notes** option on the **Status Bar** and enter the notes related to that slide in the notes pane.

Another way of adding a Speaker Note is, click the **View** tab > **Notes Page** from the **Presentation Views** group on the ribbon.

Now, enter the **Speaker Notes** in the **Notes Placeholder**, just click and enter the text in the **Notes placeholder**.

In Notes page view, you can even include images, shapes, or graphics, in the Speaker Notes.

To include graphics to the **Notes page**, do as follow:

1. Click in the **Notes Placeholder**.
2. Click the **Insert** tab > **Shapes** (to insert shape) from **Illustration** group.
3. Select the shape you want to insert.
4. Click and drag to add shape; the **Format Drawing Tools** tab appears on the ribbon. You can format the shape by changing the *Shape fill, Shape Outline, Shape Effects, and Shape Styles*, and so on.

Note: To insert the graphics, pictures, or shapes, the presentation must be in the Notes Page View only. Also, you can insert Notes in only three views: Normal View, Outline View and Notes Page View.

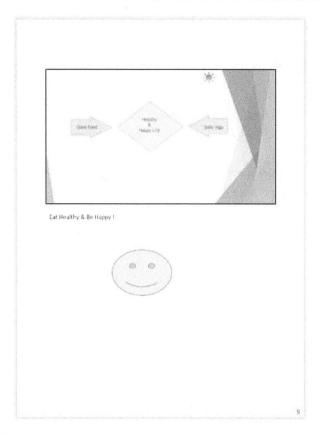

To insert images, click the **Insert** tab > **Images** group > **Pictures**; it opens the **Insert Picture** dialog. Select the image from your pc and click the **OK** button.

Preparing Handouts

Occasionally, you may want to give your audience a handout to take notes. You can use the handout feature in PowerPoint to create handouts. Handouts are used to view how your slides will look when printed. You can add Header, Footer, Date, Page Number and customize the design and layout of the handouts from the Handout Master View. You can also specify the **Page setup** options for your presentation. You can format the font of the placeholders and move and resize the other placeholders like header, footer, date, slide number.

Note: You cannot resize or move the slide placeholders in the Handout Master View.

To create Handouts:

1. Click the **View** tab > **Master Views** group > **Handout Master**; the **Handout Master** tab appears on the ribbon.
2. Click the **Handout Master** tab > **Page Setup** group > **Handout Orientation** button; it lists two options: Portrait and Landscape.

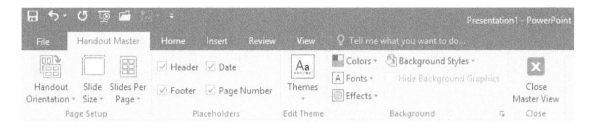

3. Select the appropriate option.

4. Click the **Slides per Page** option from the **Page Setup** group.

5. Select the appropriate option from the drop-down. For example, select **3 Slides** from the drop-down, if you want to print three slides per page for handouts.

In the **Handout Master** tab,

A. Select or deselect the **Header**, **Footer**, **Page Number**, and **Date** options from the **Placeholders** group.

B. Change the *Background style, Colors, Fonts and add effects* from the **Background** group.

C. Close the **Handout Master** tab by clicking the **Close Master View** button.

To format the background of the handouts:

1. Click the **Handout Master** tab > **Background** group > **Background Style**.
2. Select the background from the gallery (or) click the **Format Background** option from the list for more background options; it displays **Format Background pane** on the right.
3. Select **Gradient Fill** option for gradient effects.
4. Set the *Type, Direction. Angle, Color, Position, Transparency and Brightness* as required.
5. Select **Picture or Texture Fill** option for Texture effects.
6. Select the texture type from the **Texture** drop down, and then select **Tile Picture as texture** checkbox.
7. Specify other settings like *Alignment, Mirror Type, Offset X, Offset Y, Scale X, And Scale Y* as required.
8. Select the **Pattern Fill** option for pattern effects.
9. Select the pattern, foreground and background colors.
10. Click the **Apply to All** button to apply the changes to all slides (or) close the **Format Background** pane to apply the changes only to the selected slide.

To format the theme colors and fonts:
1. Click the **Handout Master** tab > **Background** group.
2. Click the **Theme Colors** drop down; it lists a gallery of theme colors.
3. Select the theme color from the gallery.
4. Click the **Theme Fonts** drop down; it lists a gallery of theme fonts.
5. Select the appropriate theme font from the gallery.

Printing Handouts

To print the presentation:

1. Click the **File** tab.
2. Click the **Print** option on the **Backstage View**.
   You can view the slide show in the Print Preview area at the right hand side.
3. Click the **Print Layout** drop-down below the **Slides** box; it lists a gallery of print layouts.
4. Select the required layout under **Handouts** section. For example, if you want to print three slides per page, then select 3 Slides.

Note: If you print several slides per page on a handout, then make sure that your audience can read them without straining their eyes.

5. Select the appropriate option (Landscape or Portrait) from the **Orientation** drop-down.

You can move among the slides by clicking **Next page** button or **Previous page** button on the lower left corner of the right pane.

6. Select the required (**Color** or **Black & White** or **Grayscale**) from the **Color** drop-down. For example, if you want to print the handouts in black & white then select Black & White.

TIP: You can zoom in or zoom out of the content of the slides by using **Zoom Slider** on the lower right corner.

7. Select the printer from the **Printer** drop down.
8. Click the **Print** button.

PowerPoint prints the presentation handouts with the selected layout.

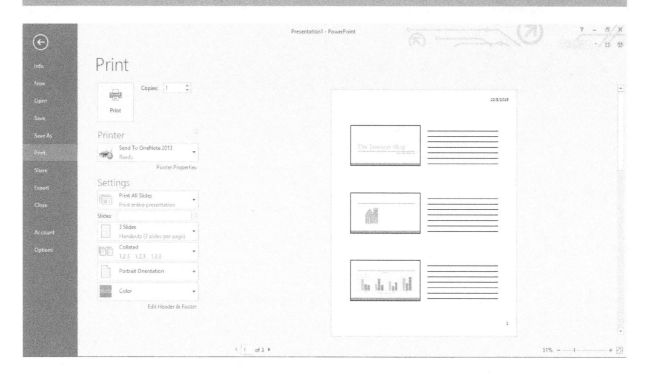

You can change the following default settings on the print page:

- Set the number of copies in the **Copies** spinner by clicking the arrows (up or down).
- Select printer from the **Printer** drop down and set the printer properties, if you have more than one printer.
- Select the slides you want to print by using the options (**Print all Slides, Print the selected slides,** and **Print the current slide**) in the **Slides** drop-down. You can also specify slides that you want to print by entering the slide numbers separated by commas in the **Slide** box. You can also enter the slide range. For example, enter 2-8 if you want to print from 2 to 8. You can also enter 3,5,6,7-11 to print slides 3,5,6,7,8,9,10, and 11.
- Select what to print from the **Print Layout** gallery. If you select **Full Page Slide**, then it will print one slide per page. The **Notes Pages** option will print one-half size slide per page with some space for Notes. If you select **Outline**, then it will print only text of the slide.
- You can print handouts by specifying the number of slides per page (1, 2,3,4,6, or 9) in vertical or horizontal order from the **Handouts** section of the **Print Layout** gallery.
- Add a frame to slides by selecting the **Frame Slides** option from the **Print Layout** menu, deselect it if you do not want a frame around the slide.
- The **Scale to Fit Paper** option on the **Print Layout** gallery is used to increase or reduce the size of the slides to fit the paper size. This option is useful if you have not set the size of the slides to match the size of the paper in the printer settings.
- Select the **High Quality** option from the **Print Layout** menu to print the slides with high quality output.
- You can print the comments and notes by selecting the **Print Comments and Ink Markup** option from the **Print Layout** gallery. It will be printed along with the slides.
- If you want to print multiple copies of a presentation, then select the **Collated** or **Uncollated** option. The **Collated** option prints the multiple copies of slides in a series. The Uncollated option prints multiple copies of slide, then moves on to the next slide.
- Set the color range from the **Color** option
- Specify the header and footer settings by clicking on the **Edit Header & Footer** link; the **Header and Footer** dialog box appears. Make changes to and click the **Apply** or **Apply all** button.

Chapter 5: Adding Pictures to Slides

In this chapter, you will learn to:

- Insert pictures
- Align objects
- Format pictures
- Arrange objects in layers
- Group objects
- Compress pictures
- Remove background
- Match properties using the Eyedropper tool
- Insert screenshots

In this chapter, you will learn to make your presentation attractive by inserting pictures. Next, you will learn to align objects or pictures, and format pictures. You will also learn to arrange the overlapping objects in layers, group objects, compress pictures, and remove unnecessary parts of the picture. Next, you will learn about the Eyedropper Tool and Inserting Screenshots.

Adding Pictures

You can add pictures stored on your computer or saved on other programs or from online. Adding pictures makes your presentation more attractive and visually appealing. You can use pictures to convey a message that a word cannot do.

You insert a picture that is stored on your computer into a slide that has a content placeholder. To do so, click the **Pictures** button in the placeholder, select the picture from the folder, and click the **Insert** button.

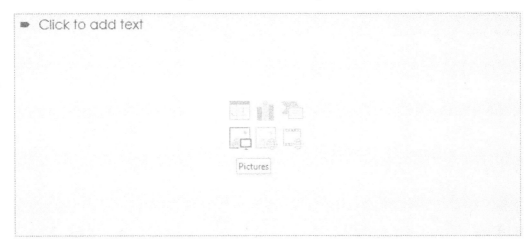

You can also insert a picture into a slide with no content placeholder. To do so, click the **Insert** tab > **Images** group > **Picture**, select the picture from the folder, and click the **Insert** button.

Adding Pictures on Blank Slides

You can even add picture to the blank slide. click **New slide > Blank** on the **Slides** group of the **Home** ribbon tab. Now you can insert picture by clicking the **Insert** tab > **Images** group > **Pictures**; the **Insert picture** dialog box appears. Select the pictures that are saved on your computer, and click the **Insert** button.

The inserted picture is surrounded by a frame to indicate that it is selected. You can use the handles on the frame to resize or rotate the picture. You can move the picture by clicking and dragging.

Adding Pictures from Online Sources

You can also add pictures from online sources. Note that you must be connected to internet to add pictures from the online sources.

To insert pictures from online, click the **Insert** tab > **Images** group **> Online Pictures** option.

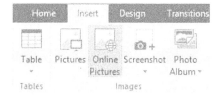

You can also click the **Online Pictures** button in the **Content Placeholder** and insert the picture.

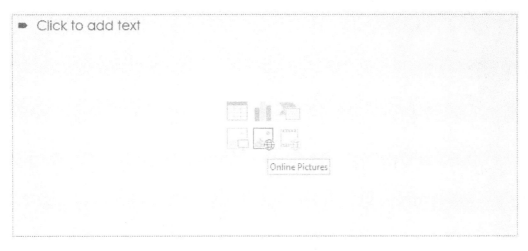

The **Insert Pictures** dialog appears. You can search for online pictures by entering the keyword in the search box or browsing the folders on your OneDrive.

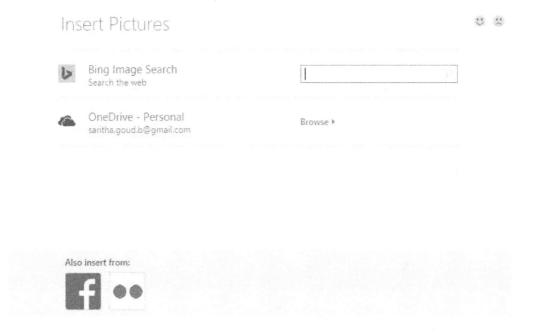

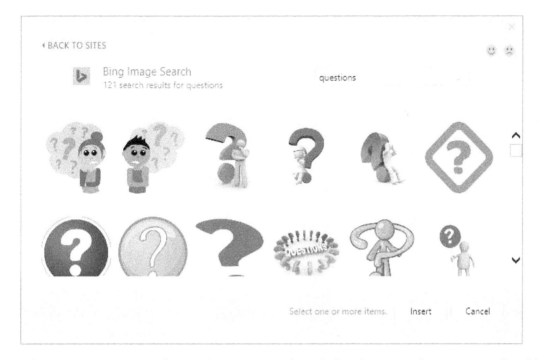

After inserting a picture from online, **Format** tab with the **Picture Tools** appears on the ribbon. You can format the picture by using tools available on this tab.

In addition to pictures saved on your pc, you can insert pictures from online sources, like:

Microsoft Office Website: You can insert clip arts such as cartoons, sketches, symbols, and photographs from Microsoft Office Website. These images are professionally designed and are license free. You can find a suitable image from this website to present a key point easily. For example, you can insert a 'Question Mark' image at the end of the presentation so that audience may be prompted to ask some questions.

Copyrighted websites: You can insert an image from a copyrighted website by taking permission from the website owner. You can also purchase royalty free images from any royalty free image website available online. Some of the royalty free image websites are:

www.istockphoto.com
www.shutterstock.com
www.fotolia.com
www.dreamstime.com

You can also find some license free images from websites such as:

www.freeimages.com
www.morguefile.com
http://littlevisuals.co/
http://nos.twnsnd.co/

http://picography.co/

Microsoft SkyDrive: You can upload and download pictures anywhere easily from SkyDrive.

Note: You can even save slides as pictures which you can insert in other documents. To save your presentation slides as picture go through Chapter 13 "Creating a PDF and JPEG File".

Formatting Pictures

After inserting picture into your presentation, you can format it by using the **Format Picture tool** tab.

For example, you can format in the following ways:

- You can apply effects like shadows, reflection, glow, soft edges, bevel and 3-d rotation.
- You can add borders to pictures with the required width and color.
- Adjust the picture brightness, contrast, and sharpness of the picture.
- Change the color of the picture to match the document content.
- Remove background of the picture by marking the areas you want to remove or keep.
- Crop the picture to required sizes.
- Rotate the picture by using the rotation handle of the picture or rotate objects option.
- Compress the picture to reduce its size.
- Reset the picture if you want to discard all formatting changes made to it.
- You can even change picture, if you want to change the picture preserving the formatting changes made to it.

Applying Picture styles

You can apply predefined effects to a picture from the **Picture Styles** gallery. On the **Format Picture Tools** tab, click **Picture Styles** group > **Picture Styles** more arrow; the **Picture Styles** gallery appears. Place the cursor on effects available on the **Picture Styles** gallery to see a preview on the image.

You can add some additional effects to the picture like *Shadows, Reflection, Bevel, Glow, 3-D Rotation, and Soft Edges*. To do so, select the image and click the **Picture Effects** drop-down on the **Picture Styles** group. A list of picture effect menus appears. Place the cursor on the menus to expand them. Select a picture effect to apply.

Similarly, you can apply borders to the pictures by clicking the **Picture Borders** drop-down on the **Picture Styles** group. Select the border color from the **Theme Colors** or **Standard Colors** section on the gallery. You can also click the **More Outline Colors** option to open the **Colors** dialog (or) use the **Eyedropper** tool and pick a color.

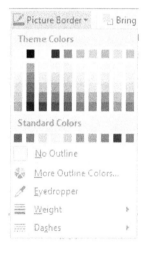

You can convert the picture to **SmartArt Graphic**, which makes it easy to arrange the caption and resize the picture. To convert a picture to **SmartArt Graphics**, click the **Picture Layout** from the **Picture Styles** group on the **Format Picture Tools** tab; it lists a gallery of **SmartArt Graphics**. Select the appropriate one from the gallery.

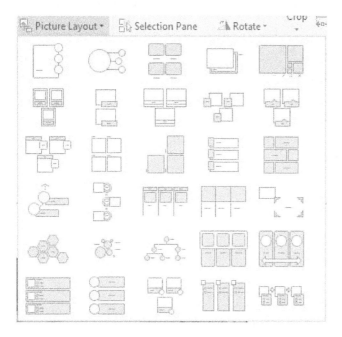

Adjusting Brightness and Contrast of a Picture

Most of the times, you want the picture to be bright and contrast so that it is easily visible to the audience. In PowerPoint, you can adjust the brightness and contrast of the picture as per your requirement using the **Brightness/Contrast** option. You can preview on the picture when you place the cursor on a brightness/contrast setting.

To adjust the brightness/contrast of a picture:

1. Select the picture, which you want to adjust.
2. Click the **Format Picture Tools** tab.
3. Click the **Correction** option from the **Adjust** group; a gallery of corrections is displayed with two sections: **Sharpen/Soften** and **Brightness/Contrast**.
4. Select any of the **Brightness/Contrast** options.

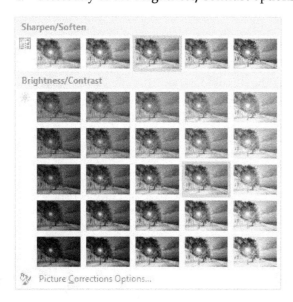

Tip: You can choose any of **Sharpen/Soften** from the gallery. click **Picture Corrections Options** on the gallery to adjust the brightness and contrast of a picture, manually. It displays the **Format Picture Pane** on the right-hand side. Under the **Picture Corrections** options, adjust the brightness and contrast of a picture, and then close the pane.

Example:

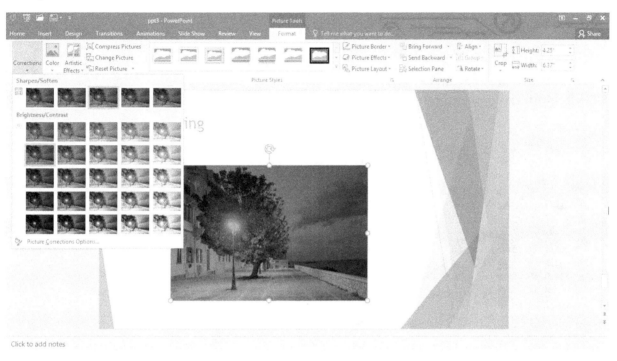

Adjusting the Color of a picture

You can change the color of a picture to match the content of a slide, improve its color tone, adjust the its color and make it visually appealing, or add effects using the **Color** drop-down available on the **Adjust** group.

To adjust the color of a picture:

1. Select the picture.
2. Click the **Format Picture Tools** tab.
3. Click the **Color** drop-down from the **Adjust** group; a gallery appears with three sections: Color Saturation, Color Tone, and Recolor.
4. Select your choice of **Color Saturation** or **Color Tone** or **Recolor**.

Color saturation is used to increase or decrease the picture saturation. It determines the amount of color in the picture. You can change the color saturation from black & white to full color.

Color Tone is used to change the color temperature of the picture from cooler to formal. The color temperature affects the actual color of the picture. For example, an increase in the temperature may slightly convert the white items in your picture into yellow.

Recolor is used to add different color effects to the picture. You can also use the **More Variations** drop-down to select from a wide range of colors.

Set Transparent Color is used to replace a color in the picture with transparency. Select this option and pick a color from the picture.

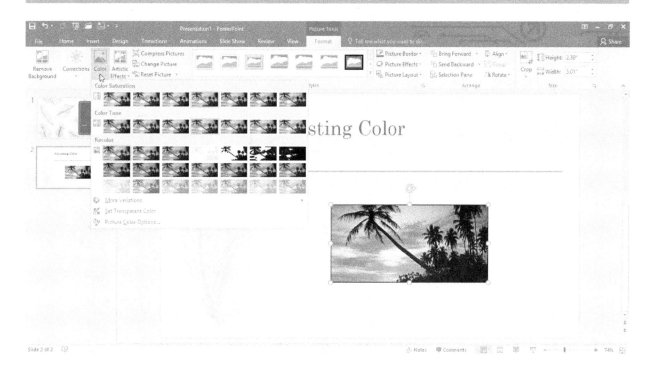

Picture Color Options opens the **Format Picture** pane with **Picture Color** section expanded. You can set the *Color Saturation, Color Tone and Recolor* the picture in this pane.

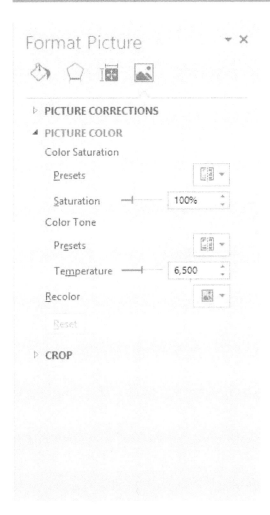

Adding Artistic Effects to a Picture

In PowerPoint, you can add artistic effects to a picture to make your presentation more interesting. It makes the slide show more attractive and gives your picture a special effect. You can apply effects like *Pencil Sketch, Chalk Sketch, Marker, Plastic Wrap, Glass, Cutout, Photocopy, Glow Edges, Cement, Light Screen, Paint Screen Paint Brush, Texturizer, Line Drawing* and so on. You can add these type of effects without switching to any other image editing program.

To add artistic effects to a picture:

1. Select the picture.
2. Click the **Format Picture Tools** tab.
3. Click the **Artistic Effects** drop-down from the **Adjust** group; a gallery of effects appears.
4. Select an effect of your choice to apply.

TIP: You can click **Artistic Effects Options** from the gallery to display the **Format Picture** pane on the right-hand side. Select the required effect from the **Artistic Effects** section and specify the settings related to the effect.

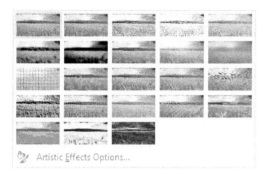

Artistic Effects Options...

Example:

Special Effects

Arranging Objects

When you insert two or more objects in a slide, they are stacked upon each other. The first inserted object will be at the bottom and the latest object will be on the top. For example, the rectangle, ellipse, and triangle are placed at the bottom, middle, and top, as shown.

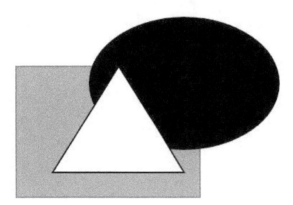

You can change the stacking order of the objects. For example, to place rectangle above the ellipse, select the rectangle and click **Format** tab > **Arrange** group > **Bring Forward** . To move the rectangle below the ellipse, select it and click the **Send Backward** on the **Arrange** group.

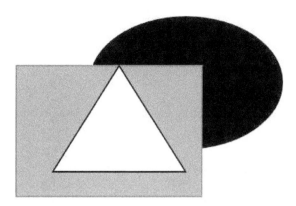

To move the triangle to the bottommost position, select it and click **Format** tab > **Arrange** group > **Send Backward > Send to Back** □. To bring back the triangle to the top position, click the Selection Pane icon on the Arrange group; the Selection pane appears. Select the Isosceles Triangle from the Selection pane and click **Format** tab > **Arrange** group > **Bring Forward > Bring to Front** □.

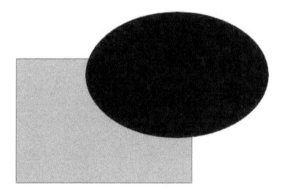

Selection Pane
It displays the list of all your objects on the slide. This pane is used to change the order of the objects and change the visibility of the objects.

To change the order of the objects, click the **Selection Pane** from the **Arrange** group on the **Format Picture Tools** tab. The **Selection Pane** appears on the right side of the presentation. In this pane you can view, list of objects, placeholders and the order of the objects with an eye icon. You can hide the objects by clicking on the **Eye Icon** or click the **Hide All** button to hide all objects on the slide. To undo it, click the **Show All** button.

You can see up and down arrow buttons in this pane, to change the order of the object select the object and click the up or down arrow button.

To close the selection pane, click the X button of the pane.

Aligning Objects

After inserting objects or pictures into the slide, you may be required to align them properly. To align an object, first select it and click the **Align Objects** drop-down in the **Arrange** group of the **Format Picture Tool** tab. The **Align Objects** drop-down consists of commands to align objects in different ways.

Use the **Align Left, Align Center**, and **Align Right** commands to align the individual or multiple objects with the left edge, center, and right edge of the slide, respectively.

Use the **Align Top, Align Middle**, and **Align Bottom** commands to align the individual or multiple objects with the top edge, middle, and bottom edge of the slide, respectively.

Use the **Distribute Horizontally** and **Distribute Vertically** commands to distribute graphics evenly within their current space.

The **Align to Slide** command is used to align graphics to the edges of the slide. The **Align Selected Objects** option is used to align the selected graphics with each other.

Grouping Objects

In PowerPoint, you can join two or more objects together. When you group two or more objects together, they can be formatted or moved as a single object.

To group the objects:

1. Select the first object and then hold shift key and select the other objects.
2. Click the **Group Objects** button from the **Arrange** group on the **Format Picture Tools** tab. It lists the *Group, Regroup,* and *Ungroup* options.
3. Select the **Group** option.

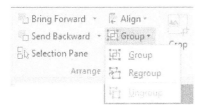

Compressing Pictures

In some cases, the picture files may occupy large space on your computer. If you insert such pictures in your presentation, it will take long time to load it. You can avoid this by compressing the pictures. Also, it will improve the quality and performance. The picture once compressed will change permanently.

To compress picture:
1. Select the picture to compress.
2. Click the **Format Picture Tools** tab.
3. Click the **Compress Picture** button from the **Adjust** group; PowerPoint displays the **Compress Picture** dialog box.
4. Deselect the **Apply only to this picture** checkbox to compress all pictures of your presentation.
5. Select the **Web** radio button for a better resolution to display on the projector and web pages (or) select the **Print** radio button for excellent quality of the pictures on printers and scanners.
6. Click **OK**.

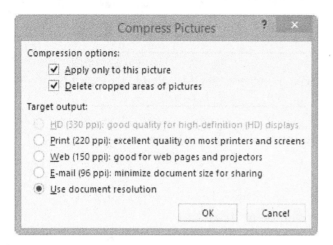

Removing Background

Sometimes, you may be required to remove the background of a picture so that you can concentrate on the main topic of the picture. In PowerPoint you can remove the background of a picture without any effort. Instead of using another program to remove background from a picture you can use Remove Background feature. This feature allows you to remove the background from a picture easily and it also saves a lot of time instead.

To remove the background of a picture:

1. Select a picture.
2. Click the **Format Picture Tools** tab.
3. Click **Remove Background** button from the **Adjust** group on the ribbon; the **Background Removal** tab appears on the ribbon.

PowerPoint automatically detects the object in the foreground.

Now you can notice only some parts of the graphic is selected and other parts of the graphic appears in violet color with handles. The violet color area of the graphic is the area to be removed.

4. Click and drag the handles to increase or decrease the area to be removed.
5. Click **Keep Changes** from the **Close** group.

You can use **Mark Areas to Keep** option on the **Refine** group to select the parts of the picture, that you want to see in the slide. click this button and draw lines across the areas to be kept.

Similarly, you can click the **Mark Areas to Remove** option on the **Refine** group and draw lines across the areas to remove.

Note: click the **Discard All Changes** button on the **Close** group, if you do not want to make any changes to the picture.

Example:

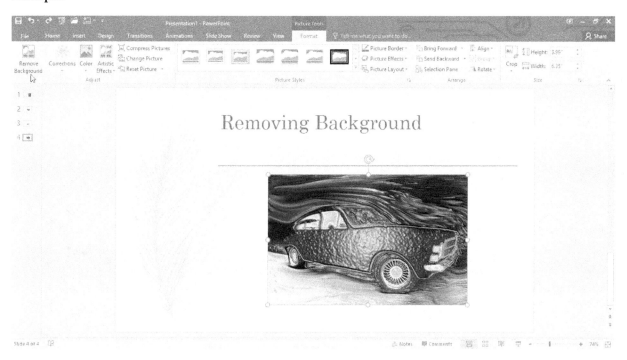

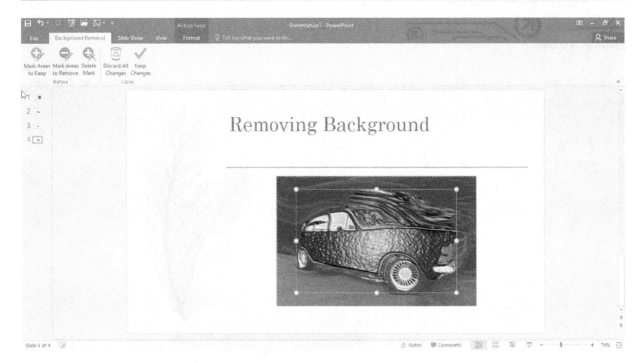

Inserting Screenshots

You can insert a screenshot from your computer in a slide of your presentation. The Screenshot feature makes it easy to take a snapshot of an open window on your computer, and insert into your presentation. This is one of the best features in PowerPoint presentation.

To insert Screenshots:

1. Select a slide in which you want to insert screenshot.
2. Click the **Insert** tab.
3. Click the **Screenshot** drop-down from the **Images** group; a gallery of windows that are opened on the desktop is displayed.
4. Select a window from the gallery; the screenshot of the selected window is inserted into the slide.

Example:

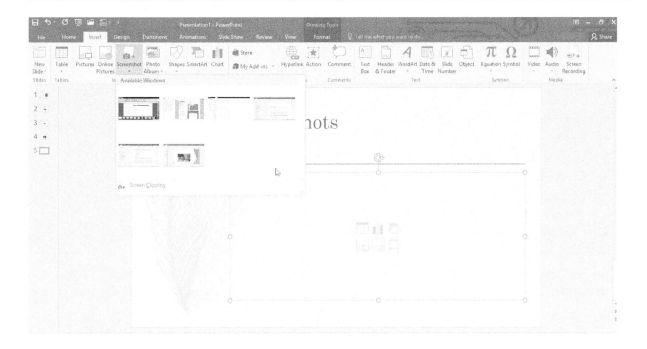

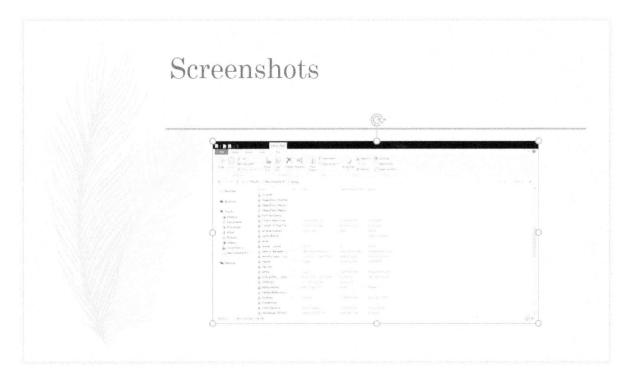

You can also use the **Screen Clipping** option available the gallery to take a snapshot of the screen and insert into the document. click this option and create a rectangle by clicking and dragging the cursor; the area inside the rectangle is captured, and inserted into the slide.

Chapter 6: Working with the Slide Content

In this chapter, you will learn to

- List the content using bullet points
- Use the Outline Mode
- Work with Word Art
- Create Text Boxes
- Create Tables
- Format Tables
- Create Tables from Excel Sheet

In this chapter, you will learn to list the content by using Bullet Points and the Outline Mode. Adding WordArt text and Text Boxes. You will also learn to create tables, format tables, and excel sheets to create tables.

Bullet Points

Bullet points are used to list the key points that you want to present in a presentation. You can use different styles of built-in bullets or create a new bullet style. For example, you can use checkmark or pictures and symbols as a bullet point in a list.

To list the content using bullet points:

1. Click the **New Slide** drop down.
2. Select anyone of the content layouts from the drop-down.

   By default, bullets appear in the **Content Placeholder**. You can use the same bullets or change them as required.

Formatting the Bulleted List

To change the bulleted list:

1. Select the placeholder containing the bulleted list.
2. Click the **Home** tab > **Paragraph** group > **Bullets** drop down.

   It lists a gallery of built-in bullets. You can see a live preview as you point any bullet style from the gallery.

3. Select the desired bullets to apply.

To change the color of the bullets:

1. Click the **Home** tab > **Paragraph** group > **Bullets** drop down.
2. Select the **Bullets and Numbering** option; the **Bullets and Numbering** dialog box appears with the **Bulleted** tab selected.
3. Click the **Color** drop down; it lists different number of colors: *Theme Colors, Standard Colors, Recent Colors,* and *More Colors.*
4. Select the appropriate color from the list.
5. Click the **OK** button to apply.

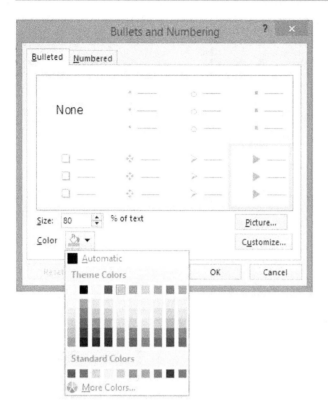

To insert picture as a bullet point:

1. Click the **Picture** button in the **Bullets and Numbering** dialog box; the **Insert Picture** dialog box appears. You can select picture from your computer or search it online.
2. Enter a keyword in the **Bing Image Search** box to search online, and press Enter.
3. Select the picture.
4. Click the **Insert** button; the selected picture appears as a bullet.

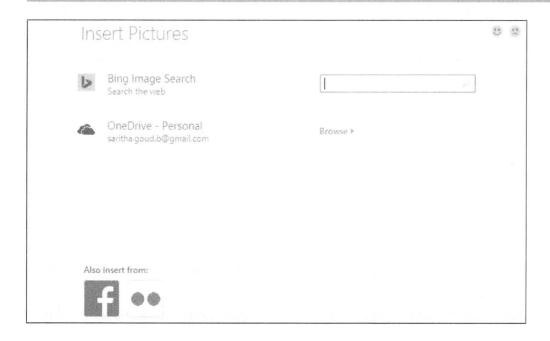

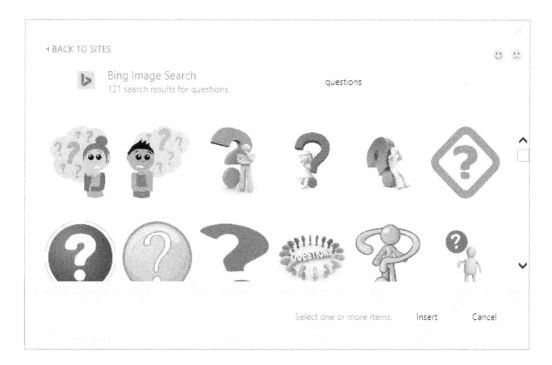

Converting Bullet Point into Diagrams

Sometimes, you may want to change the bullet points on a slide into a diagram to convey your message clearly to the audience. You can convert bullet points to a SmartArt diagram easily without much effort. To convert the existing bullet points list to SmartArt diagram:

1. Click in the placeholder containing the bulleted text.

2. Click the **Convert to SmartArt** drop-down form the **Paragraph** group on the **Home** tab.
3. Select a diagram from the gallery if it appears (or) click the **More SmartArt Graphics** command; the **Choose a SmartArt Graphic** dialog box appears.
4. Select the required diagram layout.
5. Click the **OK** button.

You can adjust the size, position and look of the diagram layout using the **SmartArt Tools**, which appear on the ribbon after converting the bulleted text into diagram.

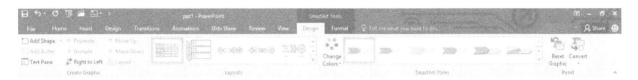

Word Art

In PowerPoint, you can create word art to add artistic effects to the text of your presentation. Word Art transforms an already existing into an artistic one by applying styles such as text fill, text outline, and text effects. You can resize, move, or format the WordArt text any other objects.

You can add WordArt to an existing text or a new one.

To add WordArt to an existing text:

1. Select the text to apply WordArt; the **Drawing Tools** with **Format** tab appears.

2. Click the **More** drop down ⌄; the **WordArt Styles** gallery appears. You can see a live preview on the slide when you point to each of the styles from the gallery.
3. Select the desired style from the gallery.

To create a new WordArt text:

1. Select the slide to add **WordArt** in **Normal View**.
2. Click the **Insert** tab > **Text** group > **WordArt** gallery.
3. Select the required **WordArt** style from the gallery.

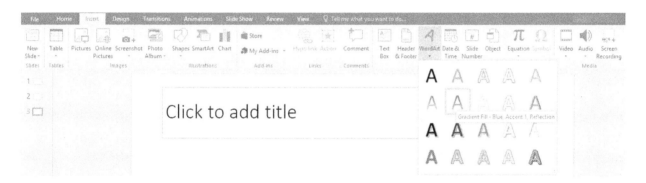

You can notice that a placeholder text (Your text here) appears on the slide, which is formatted according to the selected WordArt style.

4. Select the text in the placeholder and type a new text; the **Drawing Formal Tools** tab appears on the ribbon.

WordArt

Notice that the placeholder text appears in the middle of the slide. You can move and resize the text placeholder like any other objects. To do so, follow the steps given next:

1. Click the text placeholder. Make sure that the solid border appears instead of the dashed one.
2. Drag and place it anywhere on the slide.
3. Rotate it by using the rotate handle, which appears on the top middle of the text placeholder.
4. Click and drag the handles around the text placeholder to resize it.

Note: If you resize the text placeholder, only its size increases and not the WordArt text. The size of the text placeholder fits to the WordArt text. The width of the text placeholder can be resized but not its height.

Applying WordArt Styles and Effects

You can apply the text effects, text outline, and text fill from the commands available on the **WordArt Styles** group of the **Format** tab.

You can change the fill, color, width, line styles, add effects like bevels, reflection, shadows & glow, and transform the text wrap.

Text Fill

To apply the **Text Fill**:

1. Select the text to which you want to apply the text fill.

2. Click the **Format** tab > **WordArt Styles** group > **Text Fill.**

The gallery appears with different color options, and other commands such as **Eyedropper**, **Picture**, **Gradient**, and **Texture**.

3. Select the required color from different color options.

To apply gradient as a text fil:

1. Select the WordArt for which you want to apply gradient.
2. Click the **Formats** tab > **WordArt Style** group > **Text Fill** > **Gradient** option; the Gradient gallery appears.
3. Select one from the different gradients.

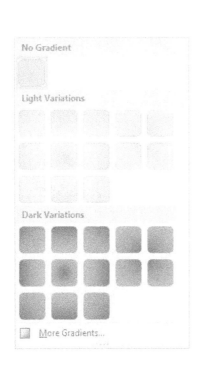

4. Click the **More Gradients** option for more gradients; the **Format Shape** pane appears on the right hand side of the window.

5. Select the **Gradient Fill** radio button from the **Text Fill** section on the **Format Shape** pane.

In this section, you can set the gradient parameters like *Type, Direction, Angle, Color, Position etc.*

6. Change the settings as required.

To apply a texture as a text fill:

1. Select the WordArt text.

2. Click the **Texture** option from the **Text Fill** gallery on the **Format** tab; it expands with a gallery of textures.

3. Click the **More Textures** option from the **Texture** gallery for more textures; the **Format Shape** pane appears on the right hand side.

4. Select the **Picture or Texture Fill** radio button.

    You can insert pictures from **File** or **Clipboard** or **Online** (only if connected to the internet). You can set the *Transparency, Alignment like Top, and Top left, Top Right, Bottom, Bottom left, Bottom Right, Left, Right, and Center.*

5. Click the **File** button to insert picture from your PC (or) click the **Clipboard** button to insert picture from clipboard (or) click the **Online** button to search and insert picture from online.
6. Select the **Tile Picture as Texture** checkbox and specify the settings to tile the image.

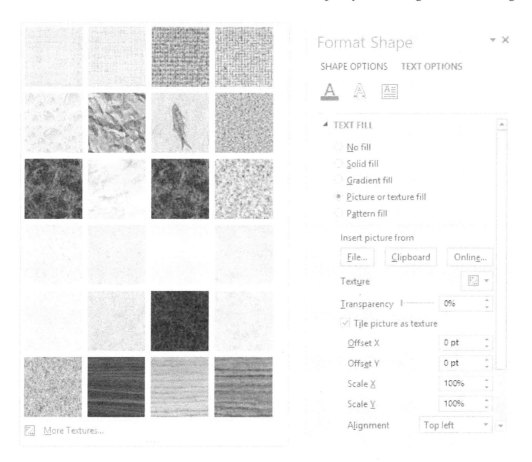

Text Outline

PowerPoint allows you to add an outline to the text.

To apply the text outline:

1. Select the text to which you want to apply the outline.
2. Click the **Format** tab > **WordArt Style** group > **Text Outline**; the gallery appears with the options such as *Colors, Eyedropper, Weight,* and *Dashes.*
3. Select the color from **Theme Colors** or **Standard Colors** (or) click the **More Outline Colors** option and select a color from the **Colors** dialog box.
4. Click the **Weight** option to expand it; various lines weights are displayed.
5. Select a line weight or click the **More Lines** option; the Text Outline section is expanded on the Format Shape pane.

6. On the Format Shape pane, select the **Solid Line** or **Gradient Line** option, and then specify your own line **Width** value.

7. On the Text Outline gallery, expand the **Dashes** option to specify a dashed outline.

8. Select the **No Outline** option from the list, if you do not want any text outline.

Text Effects

The Text Effects gallery helps you to add visual effects like shadows, reflections, glow, bevel, and 3D rotations to your text.

To apply the text effects:

1. Select the text to apply the effects.
2. Click **Format** tab > **WordArt Styles** group > **Text Effects** drop down; different types of text effects appear.
3. Expand the **Shadow** option; a gallery of shadow effects appears. There are four categories in this gallery: **No Shadow**, **Outer**, **Inner**, and **Perspective**.
4. Select a shadow type from the gallery (or) click **Shadow Options**.

The **Format Shape** pane appears with the **Shadow Options** section expanded. In this section, you can specify the options that affect the way a shadow is created.

Likewise, explore the **Reflection, Glow, Bevel, 3-D Rotation** options.

5. Expand the **abc Transform** option; a gallery appears with options to transform or wrap the text.
6. Place the pointer different transformation effects and preview the change.

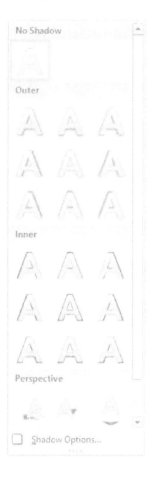
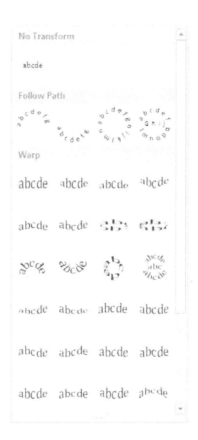

Creating Text Boxes

A text box is a placeholder identical to the one you enter text on the slide. You can resize and manipulate them as you want. By using text boxes, you can place the text anywhere on the slide.

If you want to enter text, which does not belong to the placeholders, then use thee text boxes. You can enter text in the text boxes and place them on images, shapes, graphics, or blank slides.

There are two ways to create a **Text Box**:

1. Click the **Insert** tab > **Text** group > **Text Box** on the ribbon.
2. Click the slide where you want the text to appear.
3. Enter the text in the text box; the width of the text box adjusts to fit the text.

(or)

1. Click the **Text Box** button from the **Text** group on the ribbon.
2. Click and drag a box to specify the size and location of the text box.
3. Enter the text; the width of the box remains same as specified but the height adjusts to fit the text.

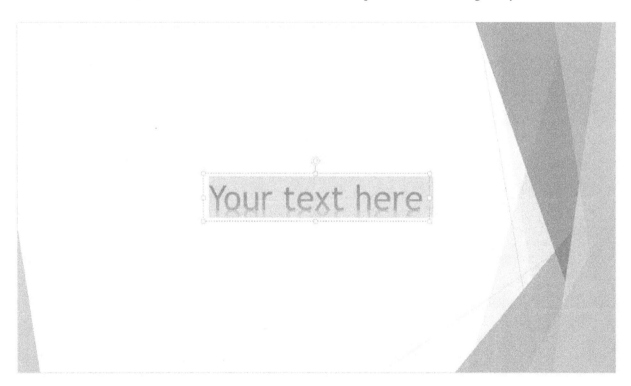

By default, the text box has no borders unless you select it. As you select the text box, you can notice that the text is surrounded by dashed border.

Click and drag the white circles called sizing handles to change the size of the text box; the width of the box changes. However, you cannot change the height of the text box. The height adjusts to fit the text that you enter by one line. You can change the height of the text box pressing Enter. You can also rotate the text box by using the rotation handle on the top.

You can move a text box by clicking on its border and dragging it. To copy and move the text box, press Ctrl key while dragging it.

There is another option to copy the text box, preserving all formatting changes. click on the border of the text and press **Ctrl + D**; the text box is duplicated.

Formatting Text Box

You can format a text box by changing its font, font color, style, outline, and so on using the commands available on the **Home** and **Format** tabs. These commands were already discussed earlier.

Altering the default format of the text box

While you create a text box, PowerPoint applies some default format settings such as font, size, style and son. You can apply your own format settings to the text box and save it as a default one. To do so, change the format settings of the text box and select. Next, right click on the text box and select **Set as Default Text Box.** The format settings will be applied to the text boxes created from now onwards.

Creating and Formatting Tables

Tables make it easier to identify and compare the individual items or categories. They help you to present a lot of data in an organized manner. This makes it easy to read the data on the presentation.

You can create a table in PowerPoint 2016, in two ways:

1. Placing the table in a Content placeholder
2. Placing the table in a Blank presentation.

To create table in a Content Placeholder:

1. Click the **Home** tab > **Slides** group > **New Slide** drop-down and choose anyone of the content layouts.
2. Enter the title name in the Title placeholder.
3. Click the **Insert Table** icon on the content placeholder; the **Insert table** dialog box appears and you are prompted to specify the number of rows and columns.

4. Enter the **Number of columns** and **Number of rows** values.

5. Click the **OK** button.

It creates a Two –Dimensional Table structure with rows and columns. The intersection of row and column is called a **Cell**. You can insert as many rows and columns as you want. The first row of the Table is called as **Header Row**, and it used to add column headings. The leftmost column is used to add row headings.

Now, you can enter the content in the Table. Use the Tab key on the keyboard to navigate between cells. click in the last cell of the table and press the Tab key to create a new row.

To place a table on a **Blank Presentation**:

1. Click the **New Slide** drop-down and select **Blank**.
2. Click the **Insert** tab > **Tables** group > **Table**.

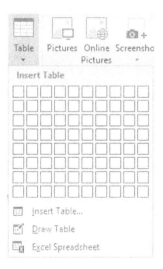

3. On the **Table** drop-down, do anyone of the following:

a) Select the row and column grids create the table.
b) Click the **Insert Table** option, and then enter the **Number of columns** and **Number of rows** values. click the **OK** button to create.
c) click the **Draw Table** option.
   i) Click and drag the cursor to draw the outline of the table.
   ii) Click **Table Tools** > **Design** tab > **Draw Borders** group > **Draw Table**  .
   iii) Click inside the table outline, hold the left mouse button, and drag the cursor vertically; a column is created.
   iv) Likewise, create a row by holding the left mouse button and dragging the cursor.
   v) Likewise, create other rows and columns.

As you create a table, you can notice **Table Tools** with **Design** and **Layout** tabs on the ribbon.

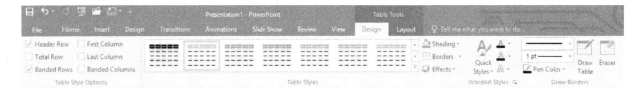

You can insert a new row above or below an existing one. To do so, click inside a cell of the row, and then click the **Insert Above** or **Insert Below** button on the **Rows & Columns** group of the **Layout Tool** tab.

Likewise, you can insert a new column on left or right side of an existing column. click inside a cell of the column, and then click the **Insert Left** or **Insert Right** button on the **Rows & Columns** group of the **Layout Tool** tab.

You can also place the cursor inside the cell and right click; notice the **Mini Toolbar**. In this toolbar, click the **Insert** drop-down and select the **Insert Columns to the left**, **Insert Columns to the right**, **Insert Rows Above**, or **Insert Rows Below** options.

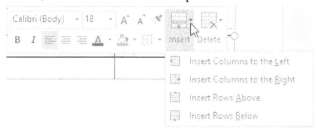

To delete a row:

1. Place the cursor on the row which you want to delete.
2. Click the **Layout Tool** tab on the **Table Tools** and
3. Click the **Delete** drop down.
4. Select **Delete Rows** from the **Rows & Columns** group.

To delete a column:

1. Place the cursor on the column which you want to delete.
2. Click the **Layout Tool** tab on the **Table Tools**.
3. Click the **Delete** drop down.
4. Select **Delete Columns** from the **Rows & Columns** group.

Similarly, you can delete an entire table by clicking in it and selecting the **Delete Table** option from the **Delete** drop-down.

If you want to highlight the Header Row, then you can select the **Header Row** option from the **Table Style Options** group on the **Design** tab of the ribbon. The header row is used to enter the column headings.

Similarly, you can select the **Banded Rows** option to highlight the odd rows of the table.

The **Total Row** option is used to highlight the last row of the table. The last row of the table is used in billing, totaling the sum and so on.

The **First Column** option highlights the first column of the table, which is used add row headings.

The **Last Column** option highlights the last column of the table.

The **Banded Columns** option highlights the odd columns.

You can select any of the above options by checking them on the **Table Style Options** group. Similarly, you can deselect them by unchecking.

Entering Content in a Table
1. Click in the first cell of the table.
2. Type the heading of the first column.
3. Press **Tab** key on the keyboard; the cursor moves to the next cell.
4. Enter the heading of the second column.
5. Likewise, enter the other column headings.
6. Click in the first cell and type-in a value or text.
7. Likewise, type data in other cells. Use the Tab key to navigate between cells.
8. Click in the area outside the table after completing the data entry; notice that the **Table Tools** tab disappears.

Formatting the Tables
When you create a table on the slide, the theme of the slide is applied to the table. As a result, the table and WordArt styles are applied to the table. However, you can format the table by adding some visual effects and background to it.

To format the table style:

1. Select the table.
2. Click **Table Tools** > **Design** tab on the ribbon.

3. Click the **More** drop down ⊽ of the **Table Styles** group; a gallery of **Table Styles** appears.
4. Select a style from the gallery.

TIP: You can a remove table style by selecting it and clicking the **Clear Table** option on the **Table Styles** gallery. The colors and formatting of the table is removed.

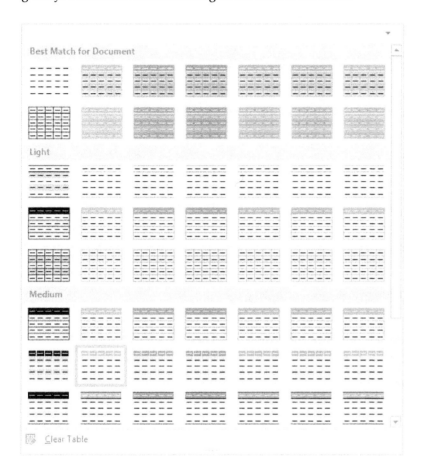

To change WordArt styles:

1. Select the table.
2. Select a row from the table. You can also select the table cells or text.
3. Click **Table Tools** > **Design** tab > **WordArt Styles** group > **Quick Styles** drop down; a gallery of WordArt Styles appears.
4. Select the desired style from the gallery.

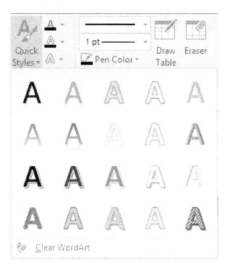

TIP: You can clear the previously applied WordArt Style, by clicking the **Clear WordArt** option on the gallery.

To apply borders:

1. Select the entire table.
2. Click **Table Tools > Design** tab > **Table Styles** group > **Borders** drop down.

   A gallery appears with options such as **No Borders, Outside Borders, All Borders, Inside Borders, Top Border, Bottom Border, Left Border, Right Border, Inside Horizontal Border, Inside Vertical Border, Diagonal up Border**, and **Diagonal Down Border.**

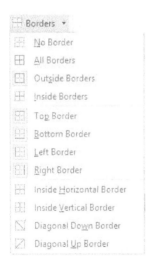

3. Select a border type from the gallery.

Note: If you click inside a cell and select a border type, the border is applied to that particular cell only.

To apply the shadings:

1. Select the entire table.
2. Click **Table Tools** > **Design** tab > **Table Styles** group **> Shading** drop down.
3. Do anyone of the following:
    a. Select the required color, gradient, or texture from the gallery.
    b. Click the **Picture** option and insert a picture.
    c. Click the **Eyedropper** option and select a color from the screen.
    d. Click the **More Fill colors** option; the **Colors** dialog box appears.
        i. Click the **Standard** tab or **Custom** tab.
        ii. Select the required color.
        iii. Click the **OK** button.

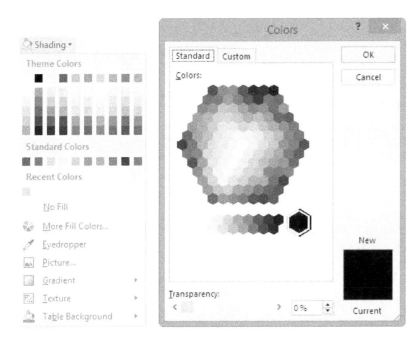

To apply Effects**:**

1. Select the table.
2. Click the **Effects** drop-down on the **Table Styles** group of the **Design** tab; a gallery appears with three types of effects: **Cell Bevel**, **Shadow**, and **Reflection**.

3. Expand the **Shadow** gallery and notice four options: **No Shadow, Inner, Outer,** and **Perspective.**
4. Select any option from the gallery.
5. Expand the **Reflection** gallery and notice two options *No Reflection and Reflection Variations.*
6. Select the required one.

Aligning the Text

You can **align** the text in the table using the **Align Left, Align Center, Align Right, Align Top,** Center **Vertically,** and **Align Bottom** options.

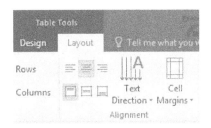

To align the text:

1. Select the content of the table or cells.
2. Select the anyone of the options from the **Layout** tab > **Alignment** group. These options are explained below.

Align Left aligns the content to the left.

Align Center aligns the content in center.

Align Right aligns the content to the right.

Align Top aligns the content to the top of the cell.

Center Vertically centers the content vertically.

Align Bottom aligns the content to the bottom of the cell.

Merging cells

To Merge cells:

1. Select the cells to combine.
2. Click **Table Tools > Layout** tab.
3. Click the **Merge Cells** button from the **Merge** group.

This will combine the selected cells into one cell.

You can also merge two or more cells into one using the Erase command. click the **Eraser** button on the **Draw Borders** group of the **Design** tab; notice that the mouse pointer turns into an eraser. Select the borders to merge two cells.

Splitting cells

To split the cells into two or more cells:

1. Select the cell to split.
2. Click **Table Tools > Layout** tab.
3. Click the **Split Cells** button on the **Merge** group; It will open a **Split Cells** dialog box
4. Specify the **Number of columns** and **Number of rows** you want to split the cell into.

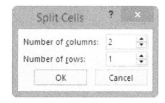

You can also Split cells by clicking on the **Draw Table** button on the **Draw Borders** group of the **Design** tab. Notice that the mouse pointer turns into pencil. Draw cell borders with pencil to split the cells.

Creating Tables using Excel sheets

There are two different ways to create a table from an Excel sheet:

1) To create a table from an existing Excel file
2) To create a new Excel table in PowerPoint.

Creating a table from Excel

To create a table from Excel:

1. Open an existing Excel file.
2. Click and drag diagonally to select the cells of spreadsheet.
3. Press Ctrl+V on your keyboard (or) click **Home** tab > **Clipboard** group > **Copy** on the ribbon.

4. Switch to the PowerPoint application window.
5. Right -Click and select anyone of the Paste options.

There are five different paste options: **Use Destination style**, **Keep Source Formatting**, **Embed**, and **Picture and Keep Text Only**.

Use Destination Style is used to paste the copied excel table as the PowerPoint table. It applies the PowerPoint table styles and formatting to table.

Keep Source Formatting is used to paste the copied excel table as the PowerPoint table. However, it will apply the Excel styles and formatting to the table.

Embed is used to paste the copied excel table as the Excel table. When you double click on it, a mini Excel file opens up in the PowerPoint. Now, you can edit the contents of the table.

Picture is used to paste the copied excel table as a picture. You can format the Picture by using the **Format** tab on the ribbon.

Keep Text Only will paste only the text of the excel table.

Creating New Excel Tables in PowerPoint

To create a new excel table:

1. Click the **New Slide** drop-down and select the **Blank Layout**.
2. Click the **Insert** tab > **Tables** > **Excel Spreadsheets**.

A new excel file opens up in PowerPoint. Also, notice that the user interface is changed. In this user interface, you can access the commands, formulas, and options related to Excel. Also, an Excel sheet appears on the slide. You can click and drag the corners of the Excel sheet to resize it.

3. Enter the data in the spreadsheet.
4. Click outside the spreadsheet to switch to PowerPoint window.

After creating table, you may want to edit it. To do so, double click the table; the Excel user interface appears. Edit the table and click on the empty area of the slide to switch back to PowerPoint window.

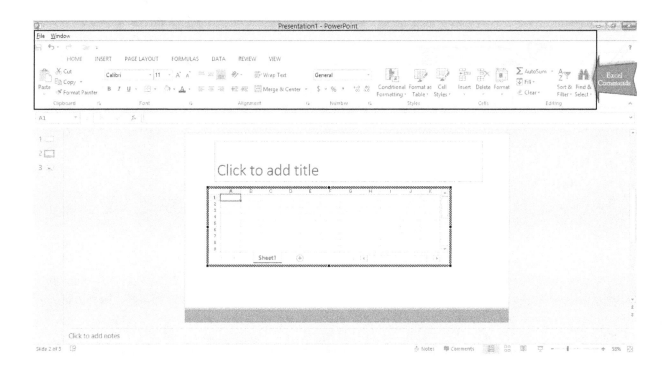

Chapter 7: Working with the Outline View

In this chapter, you will learn to

- Understand the contents that appear in the Outline View
- Enter contents in the Outline View
- Use the Promote & Demote options
- Edit text in the Outline View
- Collapse & Expand an Outline
- Export & Import Outline
- Move lists and slides in Outline

Outline Mode

Outline view is the easiest and time saving way to enter text in your presentation. It is used to organize the text in a hierarchy so that you can present your thoughts in an order manner. Also, it is used to view and edit text in your presentation.

In Outline View, you can view three panes: Outline pane, Slides pane and Notes Pane.
The Outline Pane appears on the left side of the presentation window and it displays only the text of the presentation in the outline form.

To switch to the outline view, click the **View** tab > **Presentation Views** group > **Outline View** on the ribbon; the thumbnail pane is replaced with the Outline pane. Also, you can see the text of the slides in the Outline pane. You can easily edit text of the slides in the Outline pane.

Note that you cannot rearrange the slides in the Outline pane. You can create a new slide by clicking in the Outline pane and press the Enter key. After creating a slide, you can start entering text in the outline pane.

You can also use a Word document to create a complete presentation. To do so, switch to the outline mode in the Word document and copy the content. Switch back to presentation view and past the outline in the Outline Pane.

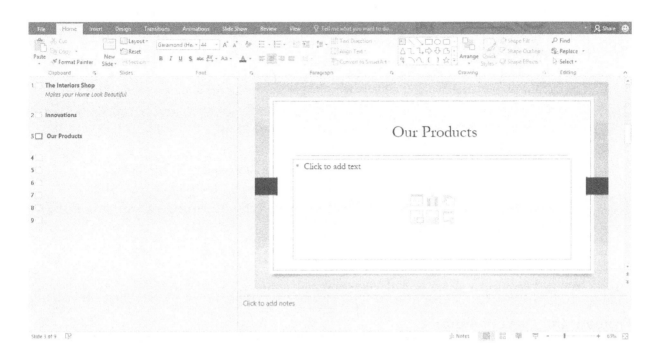

Contents that Appear in the Outline Pane

The contents that appear in the Outline pane are:

- Title and Subtitle
- Headings of the slide
- Bulleted list
- Multilevel bulleted list
- Numbered list, and
- Multilevel numbered list

The contents that does not appear in the Outline pane are:

- Shapes
- Pictures
- Graphics
- Text Boxes
- Charts
- Tables
- WordArt
- SmartArt, and
- Headers and Footers

Entering Content in Outline View

In the outline view, you can enter text quickly and easily in your presentation. To enter content in Outline View of a new presentation:

1. Start a new presentation using the Blank template or anyone of the templates available in PowerPoint.
2. Click the **View tab > Presentation Views** group **> Outline View**.
3. Click next to the **Slide Icon** ⬜ in the Outline pane.
4. Type the text in the Outline pane; the text appears on the slide while you are typing.
5. Press **Enter** key, to add a new slide (or) click the **Home** tab **> Slides** group **> New Slide**.
6. To insert a bullet point, press **Enter**, type text, and press **Tab** key; the entered text becomes the first bullet of the previous slide.
7. Again, press **Enter** key to add the second bullet.
8. Press **Tab** key to add the second level of bulleted list.
9. Now, press **Shift + Tab** key to start a new slide.

Promote and Demote Buttons

Moving a slide or bullet to a lower-level in the Outline view is called Demoting. Similarly, moving a lower-level bullet point to higher level is called Promoting. You can promote or demote bullet point or slide in the outline view using the **Promote** and **Demote** options.

To Promote the items:
1. Click anywhere in the bulleted list in the outline pane.
2. Click the **Home tab > Paragraph group > Decrease List Level** button ⬅≡ ; the bulleted list moves one level up in the outline hierarchy.

To Demote the items:
1. In the Outline pane, click anywhere in the bulleted point.

Click the **Home** tab **> Paragraph** group **> Increase List level** button ➡≡ ; the bulleted point moves one level down in the outline hierarchy and it is listed under another bullet point

Similarly, you can promote or demote` the numbered list. Notice the change in the outline pane and on the slide.

KEYBOARD SHORTCUTS:
Promote   Press Shift + Tab key
Demote   Press Tab key

Editing text in Outline

Editing content in the Outline view is similar to that in the Normal View.

To Edit text in outline view:
1. In the **Outline pane**, click at point where you want to add or delete text.
2. Type to add text.
3. Press **Delete** or **Backspace** to delete the text.

Similarly, you can edit the content of the entire slide. To do so:
1. Click the **Slide icon** ☐ in the outline pane; the entire content of the slide is selected.
2. Start typing text and notice that the entire content is replaced with the new one.

Collapsing and Expanding an Outline
If you are working on a lengthy presentation, then you can hide the contents of some slides in the Outline pane. The **Collapse** and **Expand** features help you to hide or show the content in the Outline pane.

To collapse an Outline:
1. Click the **View** tab > **Presentation Views** group > **Outline View**.
2. Select the slide which you want to collapse.
3. In the outline pane, right-click any text within a slide.
4. Select **Collapse > Collapse**; it collapses all the content of the slide and displays only the title of the slide with a wavy underline.
5. Select **Collapse > Collapse All** to collapse all slides.

To expand an Outline:
1. Right-click the collapsed slide title.
2. Select **Expand > Expand** to expand the current slide.
3. Select **Expand > Expand All** to expand all slides.

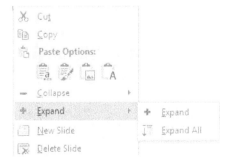

Exporting and importing outlines

You can use text of a presentation in another program by exporting it as an Outline/RTF file.

To export Outlines:
1. Open the presentation that you want to save as an .rtf file.
2. Click the **File** tab.
3. Click the **Save As** button.
4. Click **Browse**.
5. Enter the file name in the **File Name** box.
6. Select **Outline/RTF** from the **Save As type** drop down.
7. Specify the folder where you want to save the outline.
8. Click on **Save** button.

PowerPoint saves the presentation as an outline. You can use this presentation outline in any other program.

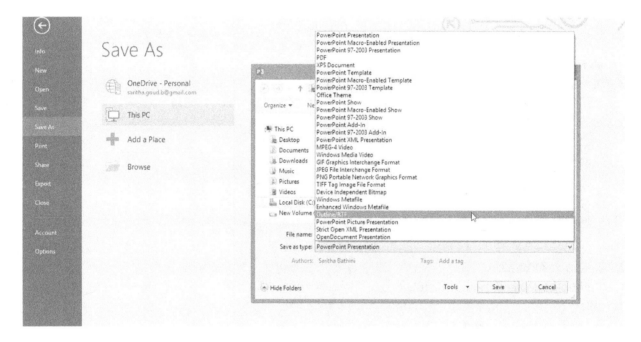

To import outlines:
1. Click the **File** tab.
2. Click **Open**.
3. Click **Browse**; it displays the **Open** dialog box.
4. Click the drop down arrow.
5. Select **All Outlines**.
6. Select the outline file.
7. Click the **Open** button.

You can notice a new presentation is opened in the Outline view.

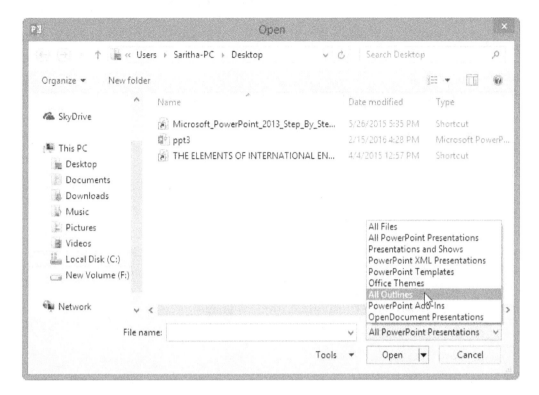

Move List and Slides in Outline

To move lists and slides in Outline:

1. Click the **View** tab > **Presentation Views** group > **Outline View**.
2. Select the **Slide Icon** ☐ that you want to move in the outline pane.
3. Click and drag the **Slide Icon** ☐ and drop it in the desired location; you can notice that the dragged slide is moved to the another location.

TIP: You can also cut, copy and paste the selected text in the outline pane.

Chapter 8: Adding Illustrations to Slides

In this chapter, you will learn to:

- Draw and format Shapes
- Crop pictures to shape
- Merge Shapes
- Insert and format charts
- Use SmartArt
- Insert Equations

Drawing Shapes

You can add shapes to your presentation to highlight the important points. In PowerPoint there are some predefined shapes which you can insert on a slide. You can select shapes from the gallery, drag, and drop on the slide. After adding a shape, you can format it by adding colors, effects, border and so on.

1. To draw a shape, click the **Insert** tab > **Illustrations** group > **Shapes** drop-down.

It lists different types of shapes such as *Lines, Rectangles, Basic Shapes, Block Arrows, Equation Shapes, Flow Charts, Stars and Banners, Callouts, and Action Buttons*. It also lists the recently used shapes.

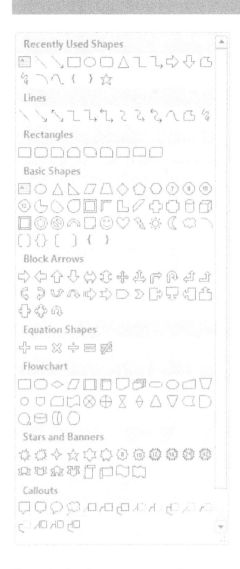

Note: Action buttons are used to run some simple actions like Back or Previous, Forward or Next, Beginning, End, Home, Information, Return, Movie, Document, Sound, and Help.

2. Select the shape from the list.
3. Click and drag to create the shape; notice that the shape is surrounded by a set of handles.
4. To resize the shape, click the dots and drag them. The white dots around the shape is called sizing handles.
5. To rotate the shape, click the rotation handle (at the top of the shape) and adjust the angle of rotation of a shape.

Note: Some shapes have yellow adjustment handles to change the shape. For example, arrows have adjustable handles that help you to change the arrow shape by clicking and dragging. You can use this adjustable handle to change the appearance of the shape without changing the size of the shape.

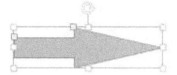

Adding Text to Shapes

You can add text to the inserted shapes to display information inside the shapes. To do so, you need to insert a text box within the shape, and then enter text in it.

To add text in the shape:
1. Select the shape.
2. Click the **Insert** tab > **Text** group > **Text Box**.
3. Enter the text in the shape.

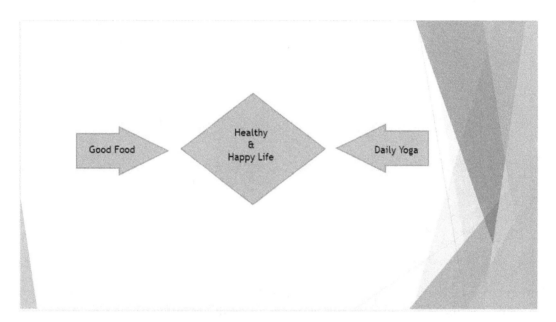

You can also add text to shapes by right-clicking on the shape and selecting Edit Text. Next, enter the text. This is an easiest way to add text to shapes.

Formatting Shapes

Formatting shapes can make your presentation visually more appealing. You can format the shape by changing the shape color and adding effects, outline, arrow styles, background style and so on. Formatting a picture is similar to formatting picture. Formatting gives a finishing touch to the shape and makes your presentation very clear.

To fill the shape with a color:
1. Select the shape that you want to format; notice the **Drawing Tools** tab on the ribbon.
2. Click the **Format** tab > **Shape Styles** group > **Shape Fill** drop-down.

3. Select the color from *Theme Colors* or *Standard Colors* or *More Fill Colors* sections.

(or)

Click the **Eyedropper** option to choose color.

(or)

Click the **Gradient** option to add gradient effects like *Light Variations* and *Dark Variations*.

(or)

Click the **Texture** option to add texture effects; it lists a gallery of textures like *Water Droplets, Paper Bag, Denim, Canvas, Marbles*, and so on.

4. Select the appropriate color or gradient or texture to apply.

To format the outline of the Shape:

1. Select the shape.
2. Click **Format** tab **> Shape Styles** group > **Shape Outline**.
3. Select the color from *Theme Colors* or *Standard Colors* or *More Fill Colors* sections.

(or)

Click the **Eyedropper** option to choose color.

4. Click the **Weight** option to set thickness of the outline.
5. Click the **Dashes** option to select different outlines like *Solid, Round Dot, Square dot, Dash, Dash Dot*, and so on.

TIP: If you click the **More line** option from the **Weight** or **Dashes** gallery, it will open the Format Shape pane on the right-side of your presentation. In this pane, you can set the *Color, Transparency, Width, Compound type, Dash type, Cap type, Join type*, and so on. For gradient outline, select the **Gradient Line** radio button and change the settings as required.

To add effects to the shape:

1. Select the shape.
2. Click **Format** tab **> Shape Styles** group > **Shape Effects**. It lists different effects like *Preset, Shadow, Reflection, Glow, Bevel, Soft Edges*, and *3-D Rotation*.
3. Click the **Shadow** option; it displays shadows in three categories: **Outer, Inner**, and **Perspective** shadows.
4. Select the required shadow effect from the gallery.
5. Click the **Reflection** option; it displays different variations of reflections.
6. Select a reflection from the gallery.
7. Click the **Glow** option; it displays different glow variations.
8. Select an option from the **Glow** gallery (or) click the **More Glow Colors** option and select the required color.
9. Click the **Bevel** option; it displays different types of bevels. Select a bevel type from the gallery.
10. Click the **Soft Edges** option and select the appropriate option.
11. Click the **3-D Rotation** option; it lists different variations of effects in three categories namely, *Parallel, Perspective*, and *Oblique*.
12. Select anyone of the effects from 3-D Rotation gallery.

Note: If you click **Shadow Options** or **Reflection Options** or **Glow Options** or **Soft Edges Options** or **3-D Rotation Options** from the respective galleries, the Format Shape pane appears on the right-side of the presentation with the settings related to the corresponding effect. You can format the settings of that effect. For example, if you click **Shadow Options** on the **Shadows** gallery, you can set the preset, color, transparency, size, blur, angle, and distance of the shadow effect on the Format shape pane.

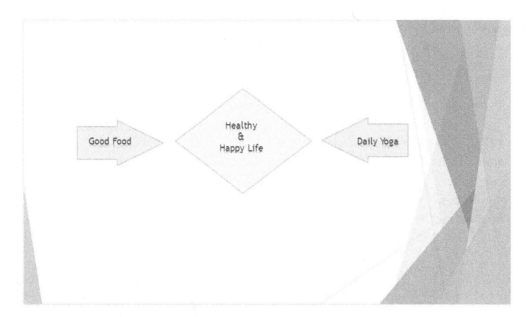

If you want to save the formatted settings for future use, then right click on the shape and select **Set as Default Shape**. Next time when you draw a shape, the present formatting options are applied to it.

Connecting Shapes

You can connect two shapes using a line by joining special handles called connection points. This illustrates the relationship between two shapes,

To connect two shapes:

1. Click **Insert** tab > **Illustration** group > **Shapes** drop-down.
2. Draw the shapes that you want to connect.
3. Click **Insert** tab > **Illustration** group > **Shapes** drop-down; it lists a gallery of shapes.
4. Select a connector shape from the **Lines** section. The connector shapes available in the **Lines** section are Elbow Connector, Elbow arrow-connector, Elbow Double-arrow connector, Curved Connector, Curved arrow connector, and Curved Double-arrow connector.
5. Click and drag to create the connector. Notice the connection points at the ends of the connector.
6. Select a connection point, drag it, and position the cursor on the first shape; four connection points appear on the shape.
7. Place the end point of the connector on anyone of the connection points; the connection is established and a green dot displayed.
8. Likewise, connect the other end point of the connector to the other shape.

Note: If white handles appear instead of green handles, then it means that the shapes are not connected.

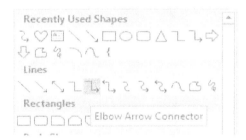

Cropping Pictures to Shape

In PowerPoint 2016, you can crop Pictures to different kinds of Shapes.

To crop picture to shape:

1. Click the **Insert** tab > **Images** group > **Pictures**; it opens the **Insert Picture** dialog box.
2. Select the picture from your PC and click the **Insert** Button.
3. Click the **Format** tab > **Size** group > **Crop** drop down.

4. Expand the **Crop to Shape** gallery.
5. Select the required shape from the gallery to crop the picture to that shape; notice the handles around the picture.
6. Click and drag the handles to resize the picture.

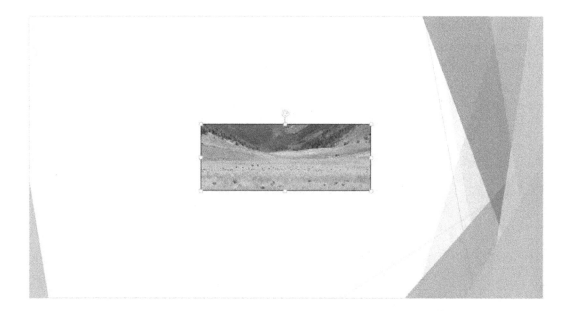

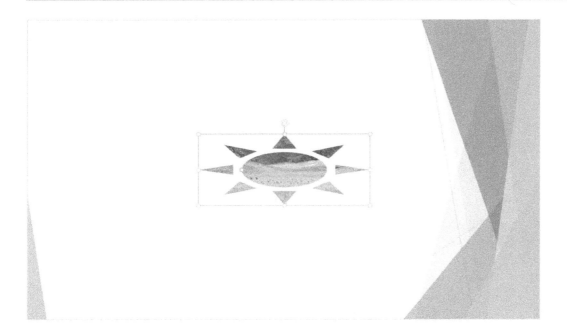

Note: Some shapes have yellow handles, which help you to adjust the shape.

Merging Shapes

In PowerPoint, you can design and create your own shapes and merge them using **Merge** option. You can also merge objects like geometric shapes, pictures, and clip art.

This example uses some shapes to draw a house by using triangle and rectangle.

To merge the shapes:
1. Select the shapes that you want to merge by holding Shift key.
2. Click the **Format** tab > **Insert Shapes** group **> Merge Shapes**; it lists five different merge options namely, Union, Combine, Fragment, Intersect, and Subtract.
3. Select **Union** option; it merges the selected shapes;

The merged shape works like an individual shape. You can format this individual shape as a unit.

Inserting Charts

You can use charts to display statistical data such as yearly or monthly growth of sales, expenditure, and so on. Charts help you to present your statistical data to the audience in a graphical format. Using charts makes your presentation more interesting and appealing.

To plot charts in PowerPoint:
1. Click the **New Slide** drop-down and select any slide layout.
2. Enter the title name in the title placeholder.
3. Click the **Insert Chart** icon on the content placeholder; the **Insert Chart** dialog box appears. It has different types of charts on the left pane, and each of the type have different variations.

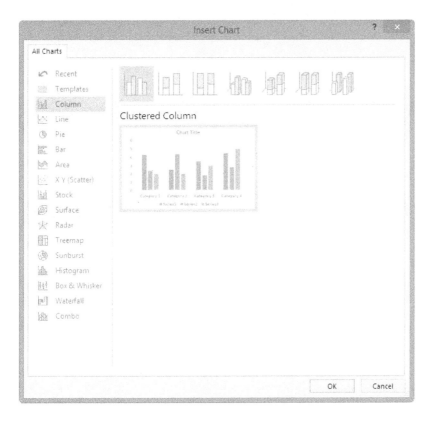

4. Select anyone of the chart type from the left pane.
5. Select anyone of the chart variations displayed horizontally; the preview appears.
6. Click **OK**; a sample chart is inserted in the current slide along with the **Microsoft Excel Worksheet** containing with some sample data.
7. Edit the data in the **Microsoft Excel Worksheet**; the data is plotted in the chart.

You can notice the **Chart Tools** tab on the ribbon as you plot the chart. The **Chart Tools** tab consists of two tabs **Design** & **Format** tabs.

8. Click the **Chart Tools** tab to format the chart.

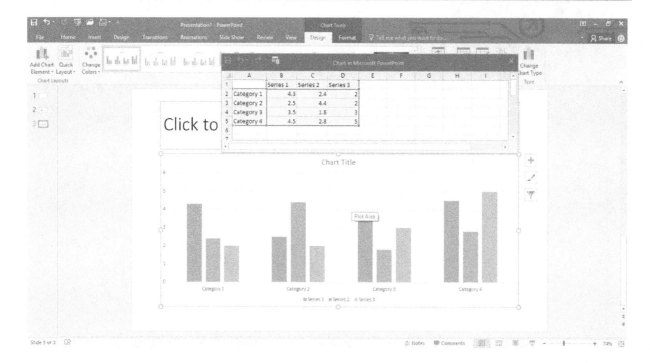

The above figure illustrates the sample column chart with the sample data in the excel worksheet.

Formatting Charts

To format the chart style:

1. Select the chart.
2. Click the **Chart Tools** tab > **Design**.
3. Click **Chart Styles** > **More** drop down; it lists a gallery of chart styles.

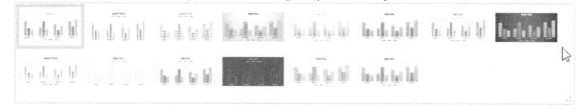

4. Select any one of the chart style from the gallery.
5. Click the **Change Colors** drop-down from the **Chart Styles** group; it lists different variations of colors in two sections: Colorful and Monochromatic.
6. Select the desired color to change the color.

To change the layout of the chart:

1. Select the chart.
2. Click the **Chart Tools** tab > **Design**.
3. Click **Chart Layouts** group > **Quick Layout**; it lists different layouts of the selected chart type.
4. Select the appropriate chart layout to change.

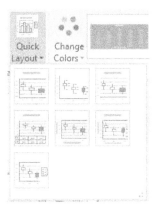

To change the chart type:

1. Click the **Chart Tools** tab > **Design** and select **Change Chart Type** from the **Type** group; the **Change Chart Type** dialog box appears.

2. Select the required chart type.
3. Click the **OK** button.

To format the chart elements of chart:

1. Select the chart.
2. Click the **Chart Tools** tab > **Format**.
3. Click the More drop-down on the **WordArt Styles** group.
4. Select the appropriate WordArt Style to apply.

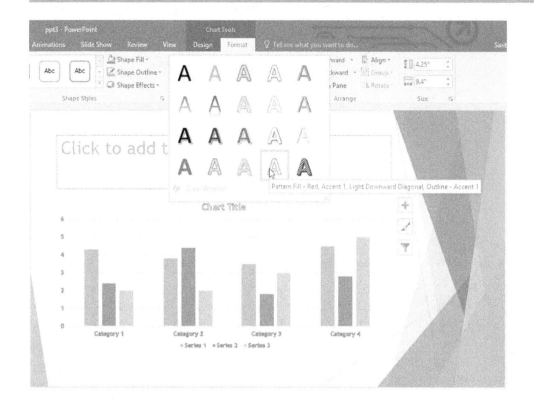

TIP: You can also select the chart elements, click the More drop down on the **WordArt Styles** group and select the appropriate style.

To format the chart theme style:
1. Select the chart.
2. Click the **Chart Tools** tab > **Format**.
3. Click **Shape Styles** > More drop down arrow; it lists a gallery of Theme Styles and Presets. You can preview the style on the chart by placing cursor on it.
4. Select theme style from the gallery to apply.

You can add chart elements like, Axes, Axis Titles, Chart Titles, Data Labels, Data Table, Error Box, Legend, Lines, Trend lines, and Up and Down Bars.

To Add Chart Elements:
1. Select the chart.
2. Click the **Chart Tools** tab > **Design**.
3. Click the **Chart Layout** group > **Add Chart Element**.

4. Select the chart element that you want to add from the list.

Edit the Chart Data
To Edit data of the chart:

1. Select the chart.
2. Click the **Chart Tools** tab > **Design**.
3. Click the **Data** group > **Edit Data** button; it opens a separate window with the data.
4. Click in the window and edit data.
5. Click the **Close** button.
6. To edit data in excel sheet, then click the **Data** group > **Edit Data** drop down.
7. Select **Edit Data in Excel**.

8. Edit the data in Excel.
9. Click the **Close** button to close the window.

Using SmartArt

In PowerPoint 2016, you can convert the text to the SmartArt graphic by using a diagram or flow chart templates. SmartArt is used to communicate information visually instead of text.

To convert text to SmartArt graphic:
1. Select the text on the slide
2. Click **Home** tab > **Paragraph** group > **Convert to SmartArt**; it lists a gallery of **SmartArt Graphics**.
3. Select the appropriate SmartArt (or) click the **More SmartArt Graphics** command on the list, if you do not like from the gallery.

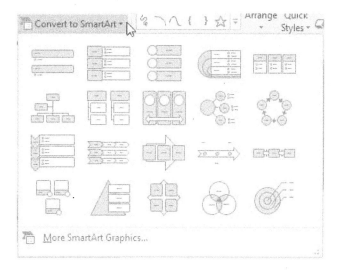

The **Choose a SmartArt Graphic** dialog box appears. It has eight categories of **SmartArt Graphics** on the left with different variations: List, Process, Cycle, Hierarchy, Relationship, Matrix, Pyramid, and Picture.

4. Click the **All** option on the left pane of the dialog box; all the eight types SmartArt's with different variations appear.
5. Select the appropriate type from the dialog box. You can notice the description and use of the graphic on the lower right of the dialog box.
6. Click **OK**.

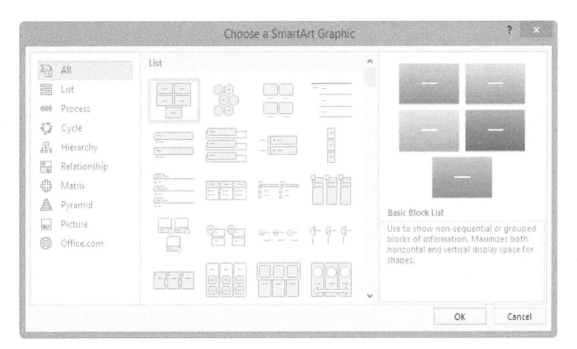

Inserting Equations

There are two different ways to insert equations:

- Typing the equation
- Selecting from the list.

To insert equations by typing:

1. Click the **Insert** tab > **Symbols** group > **Equations** button (or) click the **Insert** tab > **Symbols** group > **Equations** drop down > **Insert New Equation** option.
2. Enter the equation in the box; the **Equation Tools** tab with **Design** tab. You can use the equation structures available on the **Structures** group.

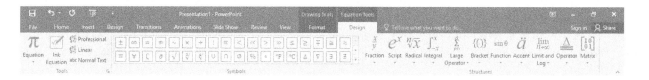

To insert predefined equations:

1. Click the **Insert** tab > **Symbols** group > **Equations** drop down.

    It lists a predefined equation such as Area of Circle, Binomial Theorem, Expansion of a sum, Fourier series, Pythagorean Theorem and so on.

2. Select the required equation from the list.

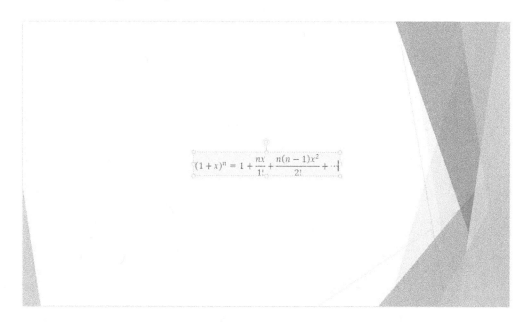

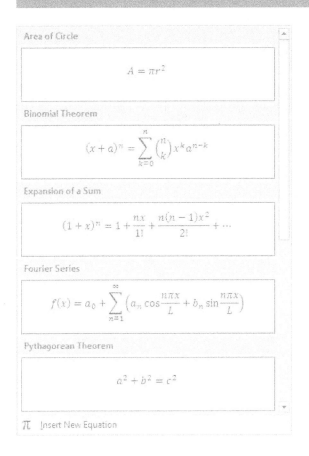

The **Design** tab appears on the ribbon. You can select the symbols from the **Symbols** group on this tab. It lists many types of symbols such as Basic Math symbols, Greek letters, Geometry, Arrows, Operators and so on.

You can select the required type of symbol from the **Symbols** group by clicking on the **More** drop down. Select the type of symbol from the drop-down located at the top right corner of the gallery; the symbols under the selected type will be displayed.

You can build your own equations by using the **Structures** and **Symbols** on the **Design** tab on the ribbon. The **Structures** group consists of Fractions, Integrals, Radical, Function, Matrix, Limit and log, Brackets, Large Operators, Scripts and Operator. You can select the required type of structure from the **Structures** group to create your own equation.

You can convert the selected equation to one dimensional or two dimensional form by clicking on the **Linear** or **Professional** options on the **Tools** group of the **Design** tab. The **Linear** option (One Dimensional) makes it easy to edit the equation, whereas the **Professional** option (Two Dimensional) is used for professional display.

You can also add normal text in the equation using the **Normal Text** option from the **Tools** group on the **Design** tab.

Ink Equations

You can insert any difficult equations of math in your presentation at any time using the Ink Equations option.

To insert Ink Equations:
1. Click the **Insert** tab > **Equation**; the **Design** tab appears on the ribbon.
2. Click the **Ink Equation** on the **Tools** group; a dialog box appears on the screen. You can use this dialog box to write the equation.
3. Click in the "Write math here" section; the mouse pointer turns into dot pointer.
4. Write the equation by using mouse; the equation appears at the top in the **Preview here** section.
5. Click the **Insert** button.

TIP: The **Ink Equations** feature is useful for touch screen devices, where you can use your finger to write the equation by hand. If you do not have a touch screen device, you can use mouse to write the equation.

There are four options at the bottom of the dialog box: **Write, Erase, Select and Correct and Clear**.

- **Write** is used to write the equation.
- **Erase** is used to erase the equation. Select this option and click on the portions to erase.
- **Select and Correct** is used to correct the equation that you have entered. Select this option and drag a selection lasso around the portion to be corrected. It lists a number of possible symbols. Select the appropriate one to correct it.
- **Clear** is used to delete the entered equation.

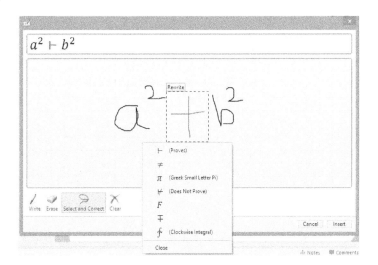

Creating Hyperlinks

Hyperlinks is a link on your document, which gives a quick access to webpages and files. It takes to you a webpage or file, when you click on it. You can use a text, object, graphic, shape, or a table as a hyperlink.

To create a hyperlink:
1. Select the text on the slide.
2. Click the **Insert** tab > **Links** group > **Hyperlink**; the **Insert Hyperlink** dialog box appears.
3. Select the **Existing File or Web Page** option.
4. Type in the URL in the Address bar (or) specify the folder location of a file.
5. Click **OK** to close the **Insert Hyperlink** dialog box.

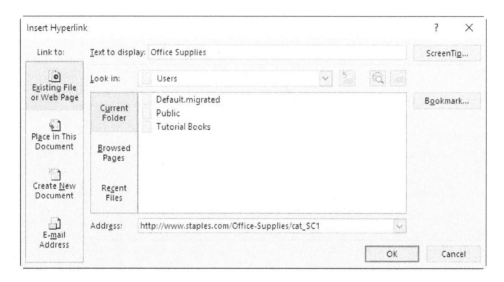

Note: If you edit the hyperlinked object, then the hyperlink is not affected. However, the hyperlink is deleted on deleting the object.

Formatting Text Placeholders

Usually, a text placeholder has no borders when it is not selected. The text on the placeholder appears to float on the slide. As you click in the placeholder, a dashed border appears and you can enter the text. Notice the **Format** tab as you click in the text placeholder. You can format the text placeholders just like text-boxes or any other shapes.

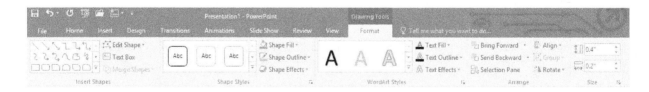

Using the **Shape Styles** group, you can format the text placeholders by:
▪ Changing the shape style of the placeholder using the predefined **Shape Styles**.

- Filling the background of the placeholder with a color, texture, gradient, or picture using the **Shape Fill** drop-down.
- Changing the color of the shapes outline using the **Shape Outline** drop-down.
- Applying effects like shadow, reflection, glow, soft edges, bevel, and 3-D rotation using the **Shape Effects** drop-down.

Using the **WordArt Styles** group, you can format the text of the Text placeholder by:
- Changing the WordArt style of the text from the **WordArt Styles** gallery.
- Changing the color of the text using the **Text Fill** drop-down.
- Changing the outline color of the text using the **Text outline** drop-down.
- Applying effects to the text using the **Text Effects** drop-down.

Innovations

Note: The changes made to the placeholder will be applied to the selected placeholder only. You can format text placeholder of all slides in the Slide Master view.

Screen Recording
To insert screen recording:
1. Click the **Insert** tab > **Media** group > **Screen Recording**. The **Record** panel appears on the screen.

2. Click the **Select Area** button from the panel; the mouse pointer turns to plus sign.

3. Click and drag to select the area.
4. Click the **Record** button.
5. Click the **Pause** button to pause the recording.

6. Click the **Close** button on the panel to stop the recording.

Chapter 9: Adding Audio and Video to Slides

In this chapter, you will learn to:

- Add a video to your slide
- Format videos
- Trim videos
- Add and trim audio

Inserting Video

You can add a video on a slide in your presentation to make it more interesting. There are two different ways to add videos to the slide.

- Inserting videos from online
- Inserting videos from PC.

Adding Video from PC

To add a video to your presentation:

1. Click the **Insert** tab > **Media** group >**Video** drop down.
2. Select **Video on My PC**; the **Insert Video** dialog box appears.

3. Select the video from your PC.
4. Click **Insert** button.

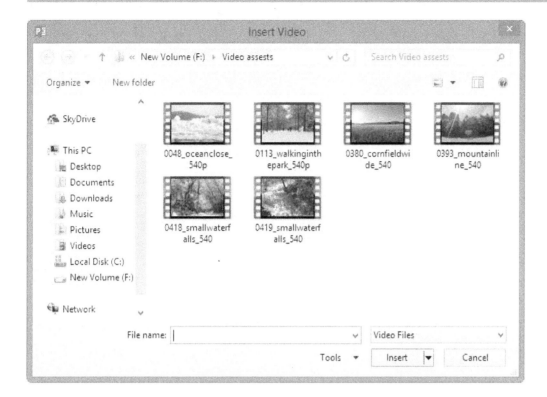

It adds video to the current slide with handles around it. You can use these handles to resize, rotate, or move the video by clicking and dragging.

You can notice the **Video Tools** tab with **Format** and **Playback** tabs on the ribbon.

Adding Video from Online

To add a video to your presentation:

1. Click the **Insert** tab > **Media** group **> Video**.
2. Select **Online Video** from the drop down (Make sure that you are connected to the internet); the **Insert Video** window appears.
3. Do anyone of the following:
   a. Click the Browse option in the OneDrive.
      i. Double click on the video.
   b. Type-in a keyword in the Search YouTube bar; related videos appear.
      i. Double click on the video to insert it.
   c. Paste the video embed code from a website.

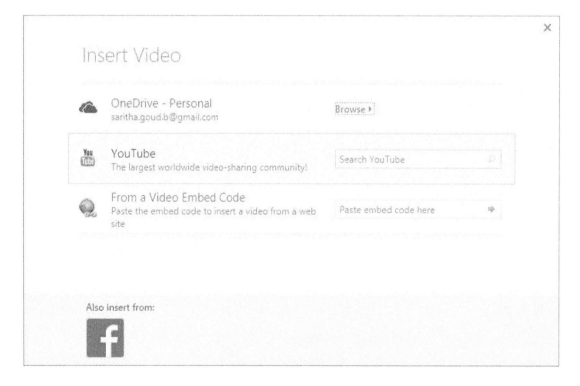

To play the video:

1. Click the **Play** ▶ button ; the **Play** button changes to **Pause** button ‖ . You can pause the video by clicking on the pause button.

2. Click the **Forward** button ▸ to fast forward the video.

3. Click the **Back** button ◂ to move backward.

Formatting the Video

You can format a video by using format options in the **Format** tab. Formatting a video includes changing color, adjusting the brightness/contrast, and applying video styles, shapes, and borders.

To format the video style:

1. Select the video.
2. Click the **Video Tools** tab > **Format** on the ribbon.
3. Click **Video Styles** > **More** drop down.
4. Select the desired styles from the **Video Styles** gallery.

To shape the video:
1. Click the **Video Tools** tab > **Format.**
2. Click the **Video Styles** group > **Video Shape** drop-down.
3. Select the desired shape to apply.

This example uses the Cloud Callout shape from the video shapes list.

 To add borders to the video:
1. Select the Video.
2. Click the **Video Tools** > **Format** tab **> Video Styles** group > **Video Border** drop-down; it displays different color options.
3. Select the desired border color to apply.

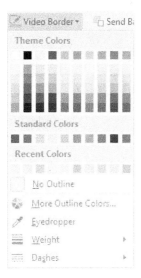

To add effects to the video:

1. Click the **Video Tools** > **Format** tab **> Video Styles** group > **Video Effects** drop down; it lists various types of effects such as Preset, Shadow, Reflection, Glow, Soft Edges, Bevel, and 3-D Rotation.
2. Select the desired effects from the list.

The following example uses **Soft Edges** effect with 50 point.

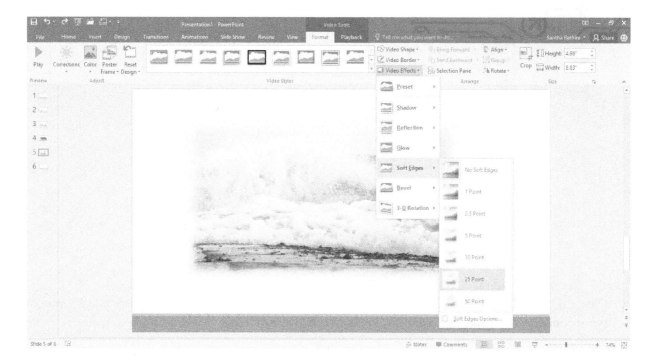

Note: You can view the **Video Tools** tab only if you have selected the video.

You can adjust the brightness and contrast of your video by using the **Corrections** drop-down on the **Adjust** group of **Video Tools > Format** tab.

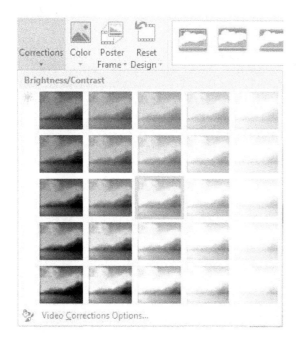

Similarly, you can recolor the video by using the **Color** drop-down on the **Adjust** group of the **Format** tab.

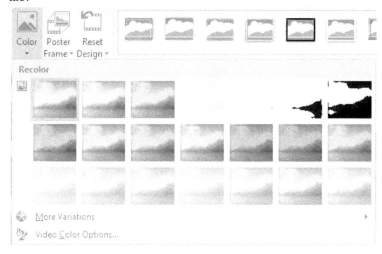

For more colors, click **More Variations**, it expands with three sections: **Theme Colors, Standard Colors** and **Recent Colors** along with two options **More Colors** and **Eyedropper**.

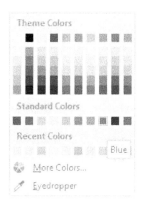

You can select the appropriate color to recolor the video. click the **More Colors** option to open the **Colors** dialog box. You can select the desired color from the dialog box and click **OK** Button. Similarly, you can select the desired color using Eyedropper option.

For more options, click **Video Color Options**; the **Format Video** pane appears on the right hand side. You can recolor the video, adjust the brightness/contrast, and crop the video.

You can set a preview image of the video clip by clicking on the **Poster Frame** option on the **Adjust** group of the **Format** tab.

If you do not want the formatting changes, which you made to the video, you can discard it by clicking the **Reset Design** option on the **Adjust** group of the **Format** tab. If you want to reset the size and formatting changes then select **Reset Design & Size** from the **Reset Design** drop down.

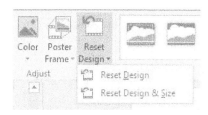

To preview the video clip after formatting click the **Format** tab or **Playback** tab > **Preview** group > **Play** button.

Trimming the Video

Sometimes, you may not want the video of your presentation to be lengthy. In such cases, you can trim the video using **Trim Video** option. PowerPoint helps you to trim the video on the slide itself, instead of using any other program or software to trim it.

To trim the video:

1. Click the **Playback** tab from **Video Tools.**
2. Click the **Trim Video** option from the **Editing** group; it opens the **Trim Video** dialog box. In this dialog, you can view the start and end time.
3. Change the start and end time using the Start Time and End Time boxes, respectively (or) click and drag the green slider and red slide to specify the start and end time, respectively.
4. Click the **OK** button.

To set the video options:

1. Click the **Playback** tab > **Video Options** group > **Start** drop down; it displays two options: **Automatically** and **On click**.

2. Select **Automatically** to start the video automatically (or) select **On click** to start the video on click.
3. Select the **Play Full Screen** option, to play the video full screen.
4. Select the **Hide While Not Playing** option, if you want to hide the clip while playing.
5. Click the **Volume** drop down and set the volume as desired.
6. Select the **Loop until Stopped** option to repeat the video until it is stopped.
7. Select the **Rewind after Playing** option to rewind the video; it reverses the video clip after it is completed.

Inserting Audio

You can make your presentation more exciting by inserting an audio clip in a slide. You can insert interesting audio clips during a slide show or as a background audio for all slides. When you insert an audio, you can view an amplifier icon on the slide.

To insert an audio to the slide:

1. Click the **Insert** tab >**Audio** button; the **Insert Audio** dialog box appears.
2. Select the audio from your PC.
3. Click the **Insert** button; the amplifier icon appears on the slide.
4. Click and drag it, to place it anywhere on the slide.

You can notice one **Audio Tools** tab with **Format** and **Playback** tabs.

Recording an Audio

You may want to play an audio or background music during the slide show. You can record an audio, insert it into a slide, and then make it as a background music for all slides. Adding an audio to the slide show makes your presentation more exciting.

In PowerPoint 2016, you can also record an audio clip using the **Record Audio** option. You can record an audio on a slide, and then play it during slide show.

To record an audio clip:

1. Select a slide in which you want to record audio.
2. Click the **Insert** tab > **Media** group > **Audio** drop down > **Record Audio**; the **Record Sound** dialog box appears.
3. Specify the **Name** of the audio.
4. Click the **Record** button ⏺.

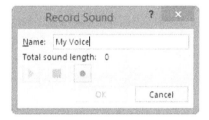

5. Record your audio.
6. Click **Stop** button ⏹ after completing the recording.
7. Click **Play** button ▶ to listen to the audio.
8. Click **OK** button.

Example:

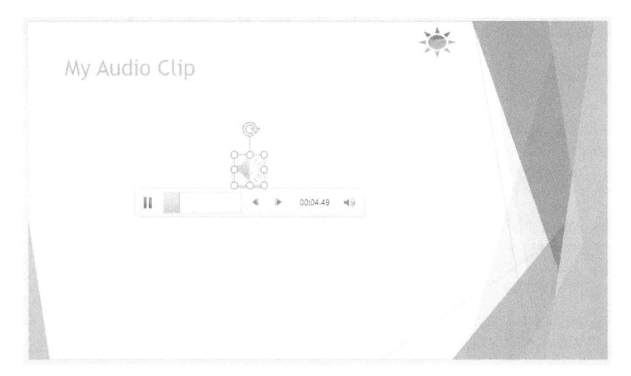

To play the Audio clip:

1. Select the audio.
2. Click the **Audio Tools** tab > **Playback**.
3. Click the **Play** button on the **Preview** group.

4. Click the **Forward** button ▸ to forward the audio.

5. Click the **Back** button ◂ to move backward.

TIP: You can increase or decrease the volume using the **Volume** button ◂» . You can also pause the audio using the **Pause** button ‖ .

Trimming the Audio

You can trim the audio by clicking on the **Trim Audio** button.

To trim the audio:

1. Click **Audio Tools** tab > **Playback**.

2. Click the **Trim Audio** button on the **Editing** group; the **Trim Audio** dialog box appears.
3. Set the start time and end time (or) click and drag on the green slider and red slider to set the start end time, respectively.
4. Click the **OK** button.

To set the volume of the audio:
1. Click **Audio Tools** tab > **Playback**.
2. Click **Volume** drop-down on the **Audio Options** group and select the required volume. You can also select the **Mute** option from the **Volume** drop-down to mute the audio.

To set the audio options:
1. Click **Audio Tools** tab > **Playback**.
2. Click **Start Audio Clip** drop-down on the **Audio Options** group.
3. Select **Automatically** option to play the audio automatically (or) select **On click** option, to play the audio on click.

To set the audio styles:
1. Click **Audio Tools** tab > **Playback**.
2. Click **Play in Background** on the **Audio Styles** group to play audio continuously across all the slide in the background.

3. Click **No Style** option, if you do not want to play the audio continuously; you can notice that all the three options *Play Across Slides, Loop until Stopped and Hide During Show* are deselected and *Start Audio clip* is set to **On click**.

Chapter 10: Adding Transitions and Animations to Slides

In this chapter, you will learn to:

- Apply slide transitions
- Modify transition effects
- Add animations
- Use the Animation pane and Animation painter
- Add animations to the bullet points

Slide Transitions

You can apply slide transitions to some or all slides to give a professional look to your presentation. PowerPoint 2016 makes it easy to apply transitions with some special effects.

Slide Transition is animation that happens between each slide when you move from one slide to another. The timing in an animation is flexible and according to the way you like it.

You can use the same slide transition to all slides of your presentation or a different transition for each slide.

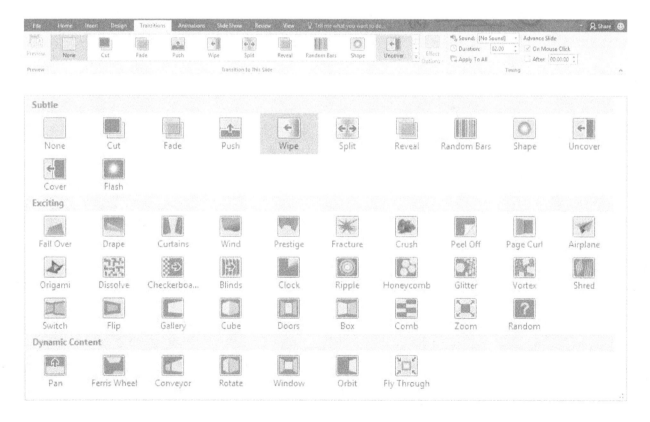

There are three categories of transitions to choose from: Subtle, Exciting, and Dynamic Content.

Subtle

These are the basic type of transitions. These are very simple animations such as Cut, Fade, Push, Wipe, Split, Reveal, Random Bars, Shape, Uncover, Cover, and Flash to move between the slides.

Exciting

These are visually appealing compared to Subtle transitions. These are complex animations such as Reveal, Curtains, Clock, Gallery, Doors, Zoom and so on.

You can use this type of transitions to the important slides only. If you use them for all slides, it will not look professional.

Dynamic Content

Dynamic Transition will move only the placeholders but not the slides, when two slides have same slide layouts. These transitions will help you to combine your slides.

Applying Transitions

You can apply slide transitions in the Normal view or Slide Sorter view to one slide or all slides.

To Apply a Transition:
1. Select the slide.

2. Click the **Transition** tab > **Transition To This Slide** group > **More drop down** ; PowerPoint displays a gallery of transitions.
3. Click the effect that you want to add for the slide.
4. Click the **Apply to All** command on the **Timing** group of the **Transition** tab to apply the same transition to all slides in your presentation. Otherwise, you can apply a different transition for each slide.

To **Preview** the slide transition:
1. Select the slide which you want to preview.

2. Click the **Transition** tab > **Preview** group > **Preview** button.

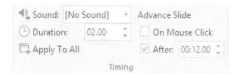

Set Time Interval for a Transition

There are two methods to move from one slide to another slide during a slide show:

- You can move to another slide manually by clicking on the slide.
- Set a time duration to move to another slide, automatically.

To specify the duration of the slide,
1. Select the slide with transition in the Normal view or Slide Sorter View.
2. Click the **Transition** tab.
3. Select the **After** option from the **Timing** group.
4. Use the **After** spinner to the specify the time to move to the next.

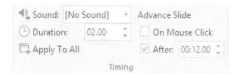

Note: If you have selected the slide with transition in the Slide Sorter view, then you can notice the time interval under the slide.

Adding Sound Effects to a Transition

You can add a sound effect to a slide transition to draw attention of your audience. Sound effects help you to highlight essential points of your presentation. Adding sound effects for too many slides may ruin the slide show presentation. You need to use the transition sounds wisely by adding them to specific slides instead of all.

For example, if you want to use transition sound for growth of sales in the month, you can use the applause sound effect.

To add sound effects to the slide transition,
1. Select a slide with transition.
2. Click the **Transitions** tab.
3. Click the **Sound** drop down on the **Timing** group; it lists different sound effects. By default, the **No Sound** effect is selected.
4. Select a sound effect to add.
5. Click the **Preview** button to hear the sound of the transition.

TIP: If you do not want any sound effect for the slide transition then select **No Sound** option from the list.

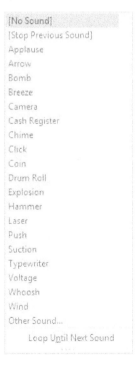

Set the Speed of a Slide Transition

The speed of a slide transition controls the frequency at which the transition effect will play. You can modify the transitions by altering the speed of a slide transition. By default, transitions are set with a specific speed, which you can change as required. You can set slower or faster transition speed as per the selected transition effect.

For example, you can slow and fasten the transition speed for Reveal and Random bars effects, respectively.

To set the speed of a transition:
1. Select the slide with transition.
2. Click **Transitions** tab.
3. Use the **Duration** spinner on the **Timing** group to set the speed.
4. Click **Preview** button on the **Preview** group to view the transition at the specified speed.

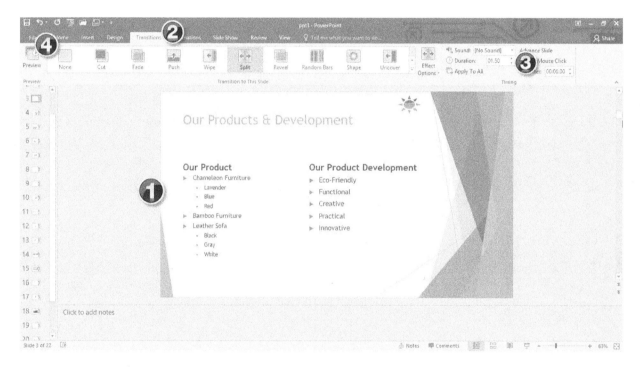

Modifying the Transition Effects

You can modify a slide transition effect by changing its direction.

To do so,

- Select the slide with transition which you want to modify.
- Click the **Effect Options** drop-down; it lists some options such as Vertical out, Horizontal in, Vertical in, and Horizontal out. The **Effect Options** vary depending on the Transition.

- Select the desired option from the Effect Options drop-down; the transition effect will modify and a preview of the transition will appear, automatically.

The **Effect Options** may not be available for some transition effects. For example, the **Effect Options** drop-down is greyed out for Flash, Dissolve, and Honeycomb effects.

Adding Animations

Animation on the slide is used to highlight a specific content of the slide and attract audiences. PowerPoint allows you add animations to the objects such as pictures, shapes, clip art, graphics, text boxes, and so on. You can add one or more animations to single object of a slide. This will help you to create a complex animation on an object.

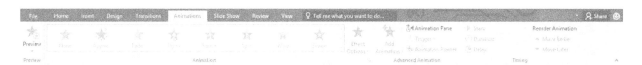

To add animation for the text:
1. Select the text or object to which you want to apply animation.
2. Click the **Animations** tab > **Animation** group > **More** drop down; it lists various animation effects which are categorized into four types: Entrance, Emphasis, Exit, and Motion Paths.
3. Select the appropriate effect.

Note: The animations are applied to a text or object. They are greyed out when a text or object is not selected.

After adding animation to an element, you can notice a numbers beside it. The numbering depends on the order for which you are applying animation effect first. You can see in the below figure.

To add multiple animations for a single object/text:

1. Select the text or object.
2. Click the **Animations** tab > **Advanced Animation** group > **Add Animation** drop-down.
3. Select an animation.
4. Likewise, add another animation to the element.

Entrance

Entrance animations are used for the introduction of a presentation. You can use this type of animation in the beginning part of your presentation. Make sure that you choose an effect which is suitable to your subject of presentation

Entrance effects are suitable to highlight the beginning of a presentation. They consist of effects such as Appear, Fade, Fly In, Split, Wipe, Float In, Shape, Wheel, Random Bars, Grow & Turn, Zoom, Swivel and Bounce.

For more entrance effects:

1. Click the **Add Animation** drop-down on the **Advanced Animation** group.
2. Select **More Entrance Effects** from the **Add Animation** gallery; the **Add Entrance Effect** dialog box appears. This dialog box is divided into four categories: Basic, Subtle, Moderate, and Exciting.
3. Select the effect from the dialog box.
4. Select the **Preview Effect** option at the lower left corner of the dialog box to preview the effect after selecting it.
5. Click **OK**.

Note: The effects of the Exciting category vary depending on the elements selected. For example, if you select a text element, all the effects in the **Exciting** category of the **Add Entrance effect** dialog box are available. However, some of the effects are greyed out when you select an element other than text.

Emphasis

Emphasis animation effect is used to highlight the important elements on the slide. Some of the Emphasis Effects are: Spin, Grow/Shrink, Underline, Wave, Pulse and so on. The Emphasis effects are more suitable to animate the text elements by changing the color and font style. Make sure that you apply this type of effects only to emphasize something in your presentation.

Note that all the Emphasis effects are available for a text element. However, some effects like Brush Color, Font Color, Underline, Bold Flash, Bold Reveal, and Wave are not available for objects such as graphics, pictures, and charts.

For more Emphasis Effects:

1. Click the **Add Animation** from **Advanced Animation** group.
2. Select **More Emphasis Effects** from the **Add Animation** gallery; it opens the **Add Emphasis Effect** dialog box with more effects. This dialog box is divided into four categories: Basic, Subtle, Moderate and Exciting.
3. Select the **Preview Effect** option at the lower left corner of the dialog box to preview the effect after selecting it.
4. Click **OK.**

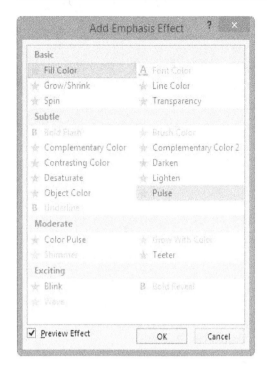

Exit

Exit Animation effects are used for the elements that are appear at the end of the presentation. There are number of different Exit effects such as Fade, Disappear, and Fly out, Split, Bounce, Wipe, Wheel, and Float out, Zoom, Random Bars, Shrink & Turn, and Swivel.

For more Exit Effects:

1. Click the **Add Animation** from the **Advanced Animation** group.
2. Select **More Exit Effects** from the **Add Animation** gallery; the **Add Exit Effect** dialog box appears; This dialog box is divided into four categories: Basic, Subtle, Moderate and Exciting.
3. Select the **Preview Effect** option at the lower left corner of the dialog box, to preview the effect after selecting it.
4. Click **OK.**

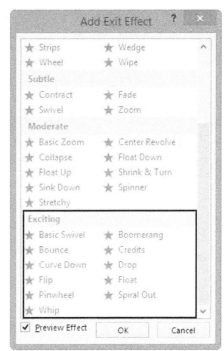

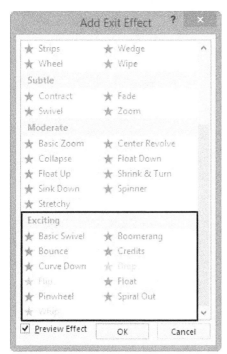

Motion Paths

Motion path animations are used to make the slide object move within the side. In PowerPoint, there are six basic motion paths: Lines, Arcs, Turns, Shapes, Loops, and Custom Path.

You can add anyone of the Paths to the text or objects like shapes, pictures, graphics and so on.

To add a Motion Path to an object like shapes, graphics, images:

1. Select the object.
2. Click the **Animations** tab > **Animation** group > **More** drop down ⬚.
3. Scroll down to the **Motion Path** section and select the required motion path; notice number beside the object and the path of the object.
4. Click **Preview** button on the **Preview** group of the **Animations tab**.

For example, if you want to add **Loops Motion Path** to the shape, then select the shape and click the Loops option on the Motion Paths section, as shown in figure.

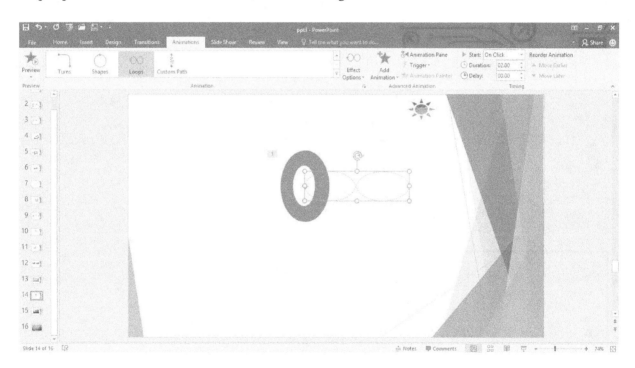

For more Motion Paths:

1. Select the object.
2. Click the **Add Animation** drop-down on the **Advanced Animation** group.
3. Select **More Motion Paths** from the **Add Animation** gallery; the **Add Motion Path** dialog box appears. The motion paths are divided into three categories: Basic, Lines Curves, and Special.

4. Select the required motion path.
5. Select the **Preview Effect** option.
6. Click **OK**.

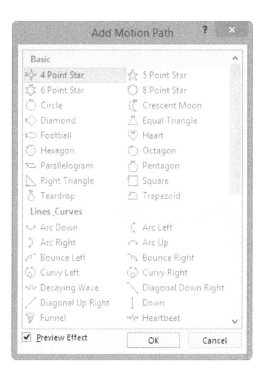

Creating Custom Path

You can create a custom path, if none of the existing motion paths suits your needs. In a custom path, you can define the start and end point of the animation movement for an object on the slide. The start location can be anywhere on the slide.

To create your own motion path:

1. Select the object for which you want to add custom path.
2. Click the **Animations** tab > **Animation group** > **More** drop down ⬚. The Animations gallery appears.
3. Select the **Custom Path** option from the **Motion Paths** section on the gallery; notice that the mouse pointer turns into plus sign.

4. Click and move the cursor to create straight path (don't drag).
5. Click to specify the end point of the line segment.
6. Double click cursor to specify the end point of the path.

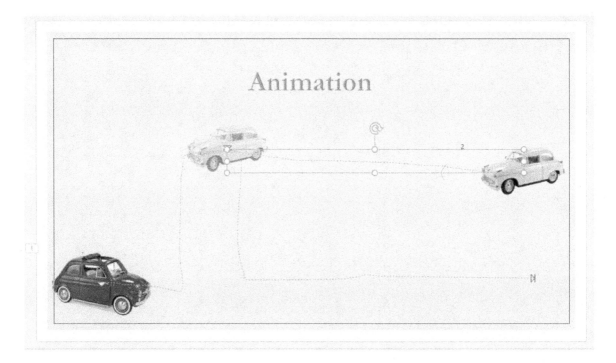

7. Click the **Preview** button on the **Preview** group to view the animation.

Animation Pane

Working with animations may require you to deal with lot of settings, and it is good to access all these settings at one place. For this purpose, PowerPoint provides you with the Animation Pane. It is used to manage animations and edit the timeline of the animation on a slide. You can rearrange the animation objects, set the timing and trigger of the animations, change the effect options, and remove an animation from the slide.

Animation Painter

For many instances, you may want to apply a single animation setting to many objects. The **Animation Painter** feature helps you to accomplish this by copying the animation effect from one object and applying to another one.

To apply the same effect to other slide objects:
1. Select the slide object with the animation.
2. Click **Animation Painter** on the **Advanced Animation** group of the **Animations tab**.
3. Select the other **slide object** to which you want to apply the animation effect.

To apply the same animation effect to multiple slide objects:
1. Select the slide object with the animation.
2. Double click the **Animation Painter** icon on the **Advanced Animation** group of the **Animations tab**.

3. Select the other slide objects to which you want to apply the effect.

Adding Animations to the Bullet Points

You can add animations to the bullet points with different effects.

To add animations to the bullet points:
1. Select the first bullet point.
2. Click the **Animations** tab > **Animation** group > **More** drop down.
3. Select the effect from the **Animation** Gallery.
4. Likewise, select the second bullet point.
5. Select the effect from the animation gallery.
6. Likewise, apply animations the other bullet points. Notice the numbers beside the bullet point.

7. Click the **Preview** button from the **Preview** group to preview the animation.

Note that same animation number will be to given to all the bullet point, if you select all them at once.

If you do not want to display animations of all the bullet points at once, you can use the Animation Pane to arrange bullet animations in a series. On the Animation Pane, select the second bullet point and click on the down arrow; a menu appears. On the menu, select the **Start After Previous** option.

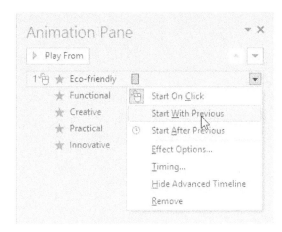

You can also select the **Start On click** option from the menu to display the bullet points on a click.

Changing Timing of an Animation

You may want to run the animation fast or slow based on your requirement. In PowerPoint 2016, you can change the duration of your animation to make it fast or slow. The time duration is the time between the start and end of the animation during the slide show. In addition to that, you can delay an animation for certain number of seconds using the **Delay** spinner. If you set the animation trigger to **On click** and the **Delay** time to two seconds, the animation will start two seconds after the mouse click.

To change the timing of an animation:
1. Select the slide with an animation.
2. Click the **Animations** tab.
3. Select an object with animation.
    You can also display the **Animation Pane** and select an animation from the Animation Pane.
4. Use the **Duration** spinner ⁀ from the **Timing** group to set the animation duration. You can also click and enter a number in the spinner.
5. Use the **Delay** spinner ⁀ from the **Timing** group to set the delay between the trigger and the start of the animation. You can also click and enter a number in the box.
6. Click the **Preview** button on the **Preview** group to view an animation after changing the time.

Reorganizing Animations

If a slide consists of various animations, you can change the order of the animations. For example, the animations of bullet points can be reorganized. You can use the move **Earlier** and **Move Later** option from the **Timing** group to change the order of the animation.

To reorganize the animations:

1. Select the slide with multiple animations.
2. Click the **Animations** tab.
3. Click the **Animation Pane** on the **Advanced Animation** group.
4. Select an animation.
5. Click **Move Earlier** or **Move Later** order options from the **Timing** group.
6. Click the **Preview** button from the **Preview** group to view the animation after reordering.

Removing an Animation

To remove an animation:

1. Select the slide with an animation.
2. Click the **Animations** tab.
3. Click the **Animation Pane** icon (if it is not open).
4. Select an Animation from the Animation Pane.
5. Press **Delete** key on the Keyboard.

TIP: You can also delete an animation, by selecting it from the **Animation Pane**, right clicking, and selecting **Remove**.

Chapter 11: Reviewing the Presentation

In this chapter, you will learn to:

- Proofread
- Rehearse Timings
- Review and add Comments
- Add Ink annotation

Checking Spelling

Once you have completed the presentation, you have to cross check for any grammatical errors or spelling errors in the presentation. Instead of using the dictionary, PowerPoint allows you to use the Spell Check feature to check your presentation for any spelling errors. You can use the Spell Check feature for your presentation to give it a professional look.

To spell check the presentation:
1. Click the **Review** tab.
2. Click the **Spelling** button > **Proofing** group on the ribbon (or) press **F7** on the keyboard; the **Spelling** task pane displays misspelled word and suggested words.

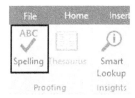

3. Select the suitable word from the suggestion list.
4. Click the **Change** button to replace the misspelled word.
    a. Click the **Change All** button to replace all the instances of the misspelled word; it will correct the error in the entire presentation.
    b. Click the **Ignore** button to leave the spelling as it is.
    c. Click the **Ignore All** button to leave all the instances of the misspelled word.

   You can notice that the spell check proceeds to the next misspelled word.
5. Repeat the steps 3 & 4 until the spell check is complete; PowerPoint displays a dialog box after completing the correction, stating that the Spell check is completed.

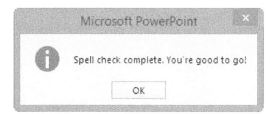

6. Click the **OK** button; the **Spelling** task pane is closed.

Note: The misspelled word appears with red wavy underline and the word with a grammatical error appears with blue wavy underline in the presentation.

TIP: You can also add the word to the dictionary by clicking the **Add** button on the Spelling task pane. In this pane, you can also listen to the suggested word to check whether it is the correct word in terms of pronunciation.

Smart Lookup

One special feature in PowerPoint 2016, is Smart Lookup. This feature is used to search for information about any word or phrase or definition. It powered by Bing search engine and make it easy to search without switching to a browser. You can also search for the word or phrase through browser, but it may distract you from the work.

To search a word using Smart Lookup:
1. Select the word or phrase which you want to look up.
2. Click the **Review** tab.
3. Click the **Smart Lookup** tool on the **Insights** group.

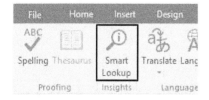

The Insight pane appears on the right hand side of the PowerPoint window with the **Explore** and **Define** tabs with definitions.

TIP: You can also select the word you want to lookup, right-click, and select **Smart Lookup** from the list.

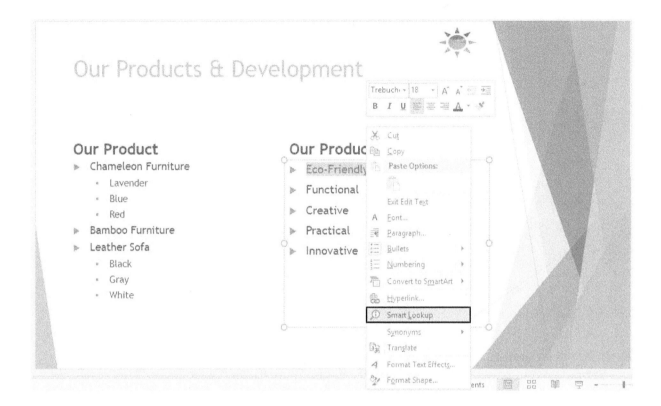

Rehearse Timings

As you practice your presentation, you can set the timing for each slide. The **Rehearse Timing** feature helps you to set the timing for your slide show and to ensure that it takes certain amount of time to deliver your presentation. When you rehearse the presentation, you can record how much time you spent on each slide. Once you record the timing, you can use it to run the slide show, automatically.

To rehearse timings, click the **Slide Show** tab > **Set up** group > **Rehearse Timings** button on the ribbon; the **Recording** dialog box appears on the top left of the slide show.

You can click the **Pause** ‖ button, to pause the recording. click the **Next arrow** → button to view the next slide show. To resume the recording, click the **Repeat arrow** ↰ button. To stop recording, click the **Close** button.

PowerPoint displays the total time for your slide show and asks you to save the recording of the slide show. click the **Yes** button to save the timing or click the **No** button.

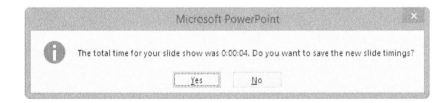

TIP: You can also right click and select **End Show** from the list while the slide show is running.

Ink Annotations

In Microsoft PowerPoint 2016, you can add freehand pen and highlighter strokes to your presentation. click the **Start Inking** option on the **Ink** group on the **Review** tab; the **Ink Tools > Pens** tab appears. You can use the Pen and Highlighter tools to highlight the key points in your presentation. There are number

of different pens and pen colors to choose. click the **More** drop down ▾ on the **Pens** group to list a gallery of pens.

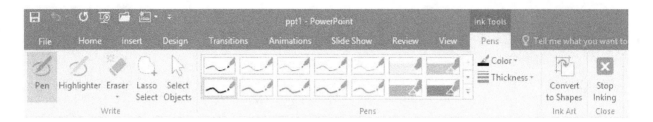

You can select the color of the pen from the **Color** drop down on the **Ink Tools** > **Pens** group **> Pen** tab. Use the **Thickness** option from **Pens** group to set the thickness of the pen from.

To erase the inking, you can click the **Eraser** option on the **Write** group on the **Ink Tools** > **Pens** tab. It lists three options: Stroke Eraser, Small Eraser, and Medium Eraser. Use the appropriate eraser to erase the inking.

You can convert the inking drawing to shape by clicking the **Convert to Shapes** tool on the **Ink Art** group of the **Pens Tool** tab.

The Convert to Shapes can convert some shapes like,

Ink drawing	Corresponding shape
Rectangle	Rectangle
Square	Rectangle with all sides equal
Diamond	Diamond
Parallelogram	Parallelogram

Trapezoid	Trapezoid
Irregular quadrilateral	Closed freeform shape with four sides.
Regular pentagon	Pentagon with all sides equal.
Regular hexagon	Hexagon with all sides equal.
Ellipse	Ellipse
Circle	Ellipse with shape height and width equal.

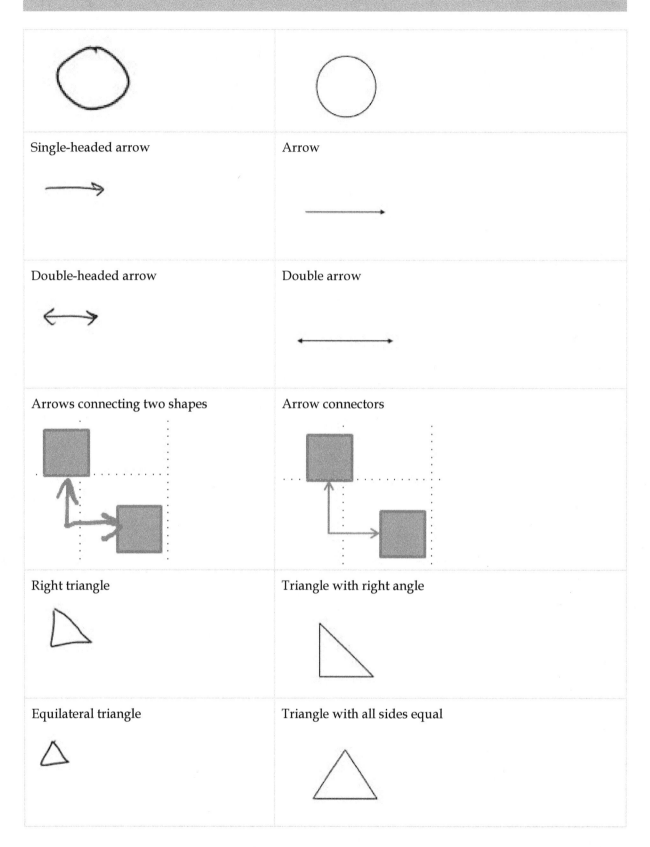

Single-headed arrow	Arrow
Double-headed arrow	Double arrow
Arrows connecting two shapes	Arrow connectors
Right triangle	Triangle with right angle
Equilateral triangle	Triangle with all sides equal

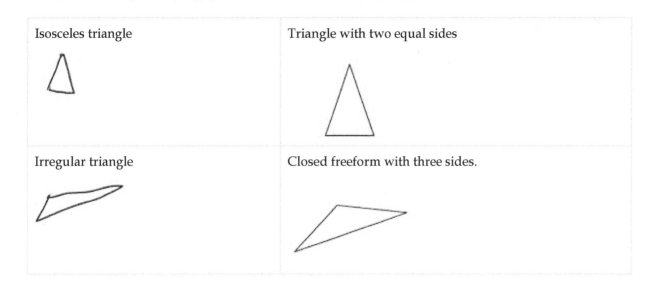

Isosceles triangle	Triangle with two equal sides
Irregular triangle	Closed freeform with three sides.

To close the tab, click the **Stop Inking** button on the **Close** group on the **Ink Tools** > **Pens** tab.

Adding Comments

You can review a presentation by adding comments what changes should be done. The Comment feature detects each comment with a comment symbol and it makes the user easy to find and read each and every comment. The comments consist of the name of the person, date and comment. After adding comments to the presentation, you can save and send it back to the author of the presentation.

To add comments to the Slides:
1. Click the **Comments** option on the **Status Bar**.
2. Click the **New** button in the **Comments** pane on the right hand side of the window.
3. Enter the comment related to that slide in the comments box.

You can also insert comments on the slides by using the Comment tool. To do so:
1. Click the **Insert** tab.
2. Click the **Comment** button on the **Comments** group on the ribbon.
3. Click the **New** button in the **Comments pane** on the right hand side of the window.

4. Enter the comment related to that slide in the comment box.
5. Click in the **Reply box** on the comments pane to reply to the comment and enter the comment.
6. Click the **Previous** button to view the previous comment.
7. Click the **Next** button to view the next comment.

8. Click the **Close** button to close the Comments pane.

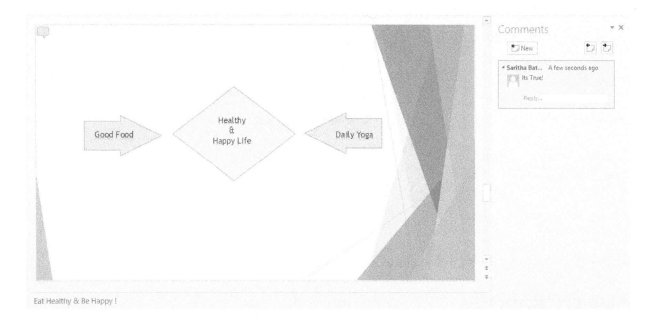

Note: As you add comments to the slides, the comment icon appears on the slide. You can click the comment icon to view and reply to the comment. Also, it opens the comments pane to show the comment.

Deleting Comments

If you find some unnecessary comments, you can delete them using the Delete Comment feature.

To delete a comment:
1. Click the **Review** tab.
2. Click the **Show Comments** drop down on the **Comments** group.
3. Select the comment that you want to delete from the Comments Pane.
4. Click the **Delete** button on the **Comments** group; PowerPoint deletes the selected comment;

Note: If you click the **Delete** button, then it deletes only one comment at a time.

To delete all comments:
1. Click the **Review** tab.
2. Click the **Show Comments** drop down on the **Comments** group.
3. Select any comment that you want to delete on the comments pane.
4. Click the **Delete** drop down on the **Comments** group.
5. Select **Delete All Comments and Ink on This Slide** to delete all comments on the present slide; PowerPoint deletes all the comments on the selected slide.
6. Select **Delete All Comments and Ink in This Presentation** to delete all comments of the presentation; PowerPoint deletes all comments of the presentation.

Chapter 12: Delivering the Presentation

In this chapter, you will learn to:
- Preview the Slide Show
- Work in the Presenters View
- Add annotations and highlight content

Viewing the Slide Show

After completing the presentation, you can view the slide show. You can start the slide show from the beginning or the current slide and end it at any time on any slide. It is advisable to start the slide show from the beginning only.

To run the slide show from beginning:
- Click the **Slide Show** tab **> From Beginning** button on the **Start Slide Show** group.
- Click the **Start from Beginning** button on the **Quick Access Toolbar**.
- Press **F5** on the Keyboard.

To run the slide show from the current slide:
- Click the **Slide Show** tab **> From Current Slide** button on the **Start Slide Show** group.
- Press **Shift + F5** on the Keyboard.

To end the slide show, right click and select **End Show** (or) Press **Esc** on the keyboard.

To view the next slide, you can click the left mouse button or press the → **right arrow** on the keyboard. Similarly, you can view the previous slide by pressing the ←**left arrow** on the keyboard. You can also view the next or previous slide show by right click and select the **Next** or **Previous** option from the list.

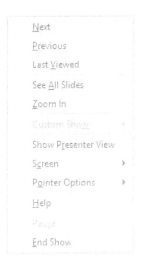

To view all slides on the screen, right click and select the **See All Slides** option while running the show. To hide the slide, select the slide that you want to hide, and then click the **Hide Slide** button from the **Set Up** group on the **Slide Show** tab.

Navigating Between the Slides

During the slide show, you can move through the slides using the on-screen toolbar located at the bottom left corner or by clicking on the screen. You can use Previous or Next arrow icons from the toolbar or press the arrow keys on the keyboard to move through the slides. You can also view all the slides at once using the **All slides** icon on the toolbar and select a specific slide.

To navigate between the slides:

- Click the **Slide show** icon on the Quick Access Toolbar to run the slide show.

- Click the **Next** icon on the on-screen toolbar to view the next slide. You can also press the right arrow key on the keyboard.

- Click the **Previous** icon on the on-screen toolbar to view the previous slide. You can also press the left arrow key on the keyboard.

- Click the **All Slides** icon to view all slides.
- Select the slide that you want to show.

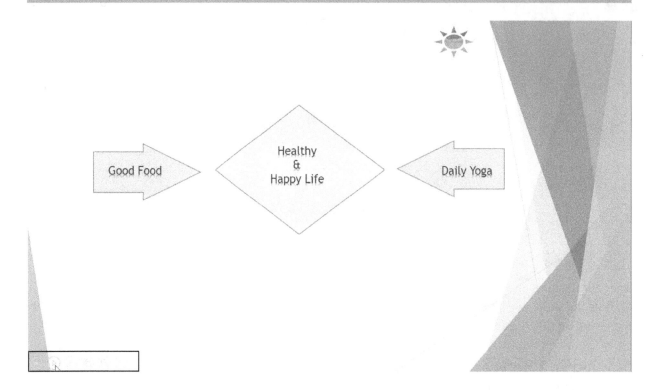

Presenter View

The Presenter View will help you to present a slide show from your computer through a projector. It is used to control the presentation on one monitor while the slide show is running on the other monitor or projector screen. It has all tools to control the presentation and is helpful if your computer supports two monitors. However, you can switch to the Presenter View on a single monitor by pressing Alt+F5.

To run a slide show on one monitor and use the Presenter view on other monitor:

1. Open the presentation that you want to run.
2. Click **Slide Show** tab **> Set Up** group **> Set Up Slide Show**; the **Set Up Show** dialog box appears.

3. Select the name of the monitor from the **Slide Show Monitor** drop-down in the **Multiple Monitors** area.
4. Select the **Use Presenter View** option.
5. Click the **OK** button.

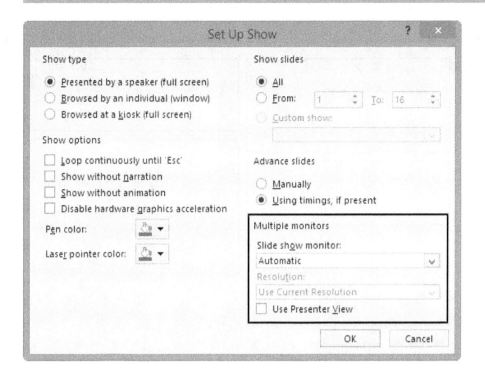

You can also set the Presenter view by selecting the **Use Presenters View** option from the **Monitors** group on the **Slide Show** tab.

In the Presenter View, you can view all details about the slides and speaker notes. You can navigate to any slide directly, keep track of the time, use the Pen or Laser pointer tools to point out important points on the slide, see all slides at once, black or unblack the slide show, and zoom in or zoom out.

In the Presenter View, you can view the next slide along with the notes on the right side. You can present the next slide by clicking on it on the right side (or) using the navigation buttons at the bottom.

Click the **Show Taskbar** option located at the top to show or hide the taskbar.

Use the **Display settings** drop-down to switch between the Presenter view and slide show.

Select the **End Slide Show** option to end the presentation.

Using the Ink tools in the Presenter View

PowerPoint allows you to use the Ink tools to highlight or annotate important points in a slide show. These tools include the Pen, Highlighter, and Eraser. You can also select the ink color. You can save the annotations after completing the presentation.

To markup any of the content with pen or highlighter on the slide during the slide show:

1. Click the **Slide Show**  icon on the **Quick Access Toolbar** to run the slide show.

2. Select the **Ink Tools** icon from the on-screen toolbar.

Laser Pointer

Pen

Highlighter

Eraser

Erase All Ink on Slide

3. Select the **Highlighter** option; notice that the pointer turns into marker pointer with the selected color.
4. Click and drag the cursor on the content that you want to highlight.
5. Press **Esc** key to turn off the Highlighter.
6. Likewise, use the **Pen** option to annotate with the pen ink.

7. Press **Esc** key to end the slide show; a dialog box appears asking you to keep or discard the changes.

8. Click **Keep** or **Discard**.

To highlight any of the content on the slide in Presenter View:

1. In the **Presenter View**, click the **Pen and Laser Pointer Tools** option.
2. Select the **Highlighter** option; the mouse pointer turns into marker pointer.

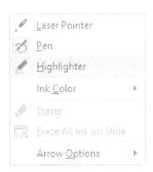

3. Select the content to highlight using this marker.
4. Click **Pen and Laser Pointer Tools** and select **Ink Color** option to change the ink color.
5. Likewise, use the **Pen** option to mark any particular content.

Note: The audience will view only the highlighted content not the tools. Only the presenter will view the tools to control the presentation.

If you want the audience to view any particular content or object: you can use **Zoom** option. click the **Zoom** option (magnifier symbol) to zoom in particular content or object. Similarly, click the zoom option to zoom out. The audience will view only the zoomed content or object not the zoom option tool. These tools are visible only in presenter's view and not in the slide show.

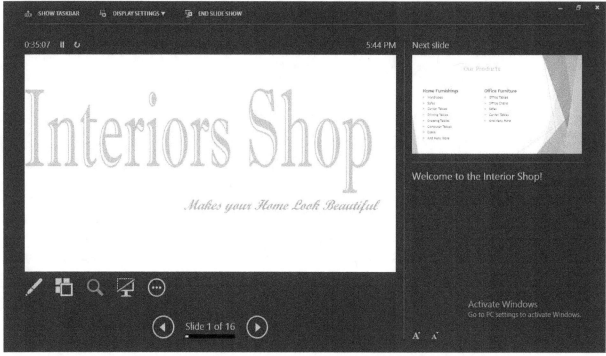

Note: You can zoom into the slide during the Slide Show also, which is explained next.

Using the Laser Pointer

The Laser Pointer tool is used to point out particular content or spot on a slide. You can draw attention of your audience and describe about the slide content more clearly using the Laser Pointer tool.

To use the Laser Pointer:

1. Start a slide show and click the **Options** icon from the on-screen toolbar.
2. Expand the **Arrow Options** menu and notice the three options: Automatic, Visible and Hidden options.
   a. The **Automatic** option is used to show the mouse pointer and hide it when it is inactive.
   b. The **Visible** option is used to show the mouse pointer during the slide show.
   c. The **Hidden** option is used to hide the mouse pointer during the slide show.
3. Select the **Automatic** option from the **Arrow Options** menu.

4. Click the **Pen and Laser Pointer Tools** icon from the on-screen toolbar.

5. Select the **Laser Pointer** option; notice that the mouse pointer ⌖ turns into laser pointer ●.
6. Move the laser pointer place it on the area that you want to identify.

7. Click the **Next** icon on the on-screen toolbar; the laser pointer ● turns to mouse pointer ⌖ temporarily. As the next slide appears, the mouse pointer ⌖ again turns to laser pointer ●.

8. Press **Esc** key on the keyboard; the laser pointer ● turns to mouse pointer ⌖.

Note: You cannot change the color of the laser pointer. It is visible on any slide background color.

Example:

Our Products & Development

Our Product
▶ Chameleon Furniture
  · Lavender
  · Blue
  · Red
▶ Bamboo Furniture
▶ Leather Sofa
  · Black
  · Gray
  · White

Our Product Development
▶ Eco-Friendly
▶ Functional
▶ Creative
▶ Practical
▶ Innovative
  ○

Erasing Annotations

To Erase the ink marks in both the Slide Show and Presenter view:

1. Click the **Pen and Laser Pointer** Tool ✐ .

2. Select the **Erase** option from the list; notice that the Mouse Pointer ↘ turns into Eraser ✎ ..

3. Click on the annotations to erase from the slide.

4. Press **Esc** key to turn off the eraser.

To erase all the ink marks in both Slide Show and Presenters View:

1. Click the **Pen and Laser Pointer** Tool ✐ .

2. Select the **Erase All Ink on Slide** option from the list.

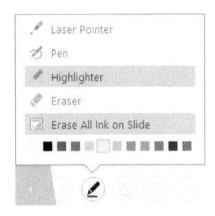

Example:

Zoom into the Slide

You can magnify the important information on your slide using the Zoom tool on the on-screen toolbar. Magnifying the content of the slide makes it clearly visible to the audience without straining their eyes.

To zoom into the slide during the slide show:

1. Start a slide show and click the **Zoom** icon on the on-screen toolbar; notice that the Mouse Pointer turns into Magnifier Glass showing the zoom area.

2. Click on the area to zoom in; PowerPoint zooms into the selected area. Also, the Magnifier Glass turns into the Zoom Hand .

3. Click and drag the zoom hand to pan the zoom area.

4. Press **Esc** key to return to the slide show view.

Example:

Interiors Shop

Makes your Home Look Beautiful

Recording Narrations

You can record audio narrations, laser pointer gestures, and animation timings for playback and slide during a slide show.

To record audio narrations:

1. Click the **Record Slide Show** on the **Set Up** group of the **Slide Show** tab.
2. Select **Start Recording from Beginning** to open the **Record Slide Show** dialog box.

This dialog box has two options: **Slide and animation timings** and **Narrations and laser pointer**.

3. Select the **Slide and animation timings** option to record only the slide and animation timings.
4. Select the **Narrations and laser Pointer** option to record the Narrations and laser pointer.
5. Click the **Start Recording** button; the slide show starts and the **Recording** dialog box appears at the top left corner.

The Recording dialog box records all the narrations and slides. You can pause the recording by clicking on the **Pause** button. click the **Next** → button and you can repeat the same by clicking on the **Repeat** ↻ button. click the **Close** button to close the recording.

After ending the slide show, you can view the volume icon at the bottom right corner on each slide of the presentation.

To delete the recorded slide show:
1. Click the **Slide Show** tab **> Set Up** group **> Record Slide Show** option.
2. Select **Clear** option; it displays four options: **Clear Timing on Current Slide**, **Clear Timing on All Slides**, **Clear Narration on Current Slide**, and **Clear Narration on All Slides**.

Clear Timing on Current Slide
Clear Timings on All Slides
Clear Narration on Current Slide
Clear Narrations on All Slides

3. Select **Clear Timing on Current Slide** to delete the recorded timing on the current slide.
4. Select **Clear Timing on All Slides** to delete the recorded timings on all slides.
5. Select **Clear Narration on Current Slide** to delete the narration on the current slide.
6. Select **Clear Narration on All Slides** to delete the narration on all slides.

Custom Slide Show

You may face a situation where you cannot show the entire presentation to all the audience. For example, you may want to show some portion of the presentation to a particular group of audience and rest to another group. For this purpose, you can create a custom slide which suites your requirement.

To create a custom slide show:
1. Click the **Slide Show** tab.
2. Click **Custom Slide Show > Custom Shows** on **Start Slide Show** group; the **Custom Shows** dialog box appears.

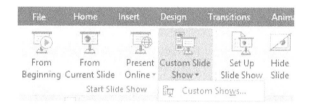

3. Click **New**; the **Define Custom Show** dialog box appears.
4. Enter the slide show name in the **Slide Show name** textbox.
5. Select the slides that you want in your custom slide show.

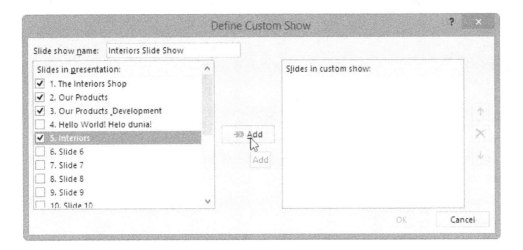

6. Click the **Add** button; the selected slides are added to the Custom Show list.

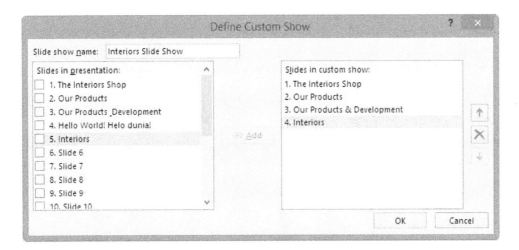

7. Click the **OK** button; notice that the PowerPoint adds the custom show to the list.

8. Click the **Close** button.

To run the Custom Slide show:
1. Click the **Slide Show** tab.

2. Click the **Custom Slide Show** on the **Start Slide Show** group; it lists the custom shows that you have created for the presentation.

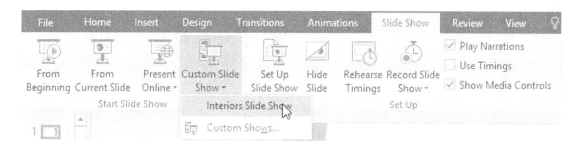

3. Select the custom show that you want to present.

Chapter 13: Reusing and Sharing Presentations

In this chapter, you will learn to:

- Create Custom Themes
- Custom Templates
- Print the presentation
- Record and Narrate your presentation
- Save your presentation as a Video
- Save your presentation as a PDF or JPEG File
- Share the presentation
- Inspect the document

Custom Theme

You can create your own themes in PowerPoint 2016.

To create a Custom Theme:

1. Click the **Design** tab > **Themes** > **More** drop-down .
2. Select **Save Current Theme**; the **Save Current Theme** dialog box appears.
3. Enter the **File name.**
4. Click the **Save** button.

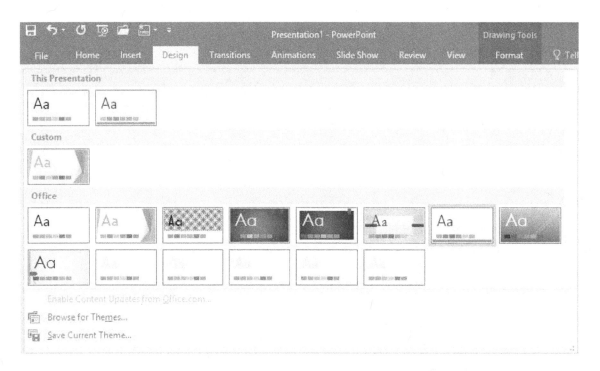

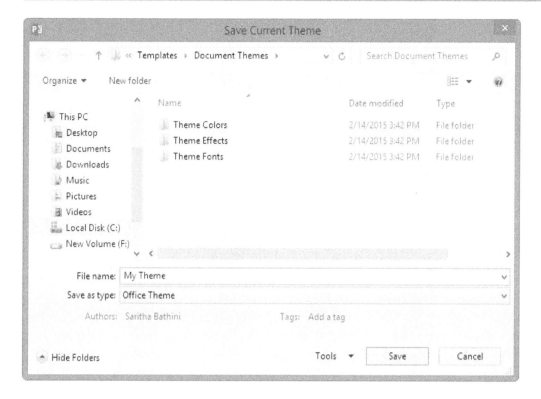

Now, close the PowerPoint window and open it again. You can notice that the theme, which you have saved, will appear under **Custom Themes**.

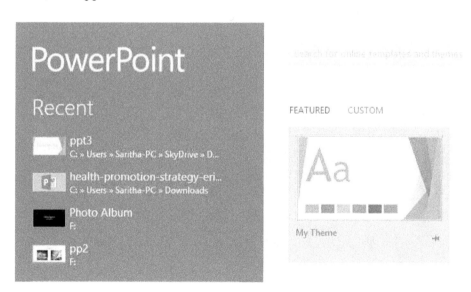

Now, you can create a new presentation by selecting the custom them from the Custom section, and clicking the Create button.

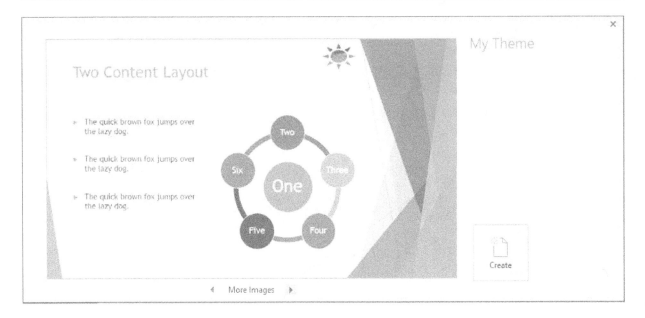

You can also view this theme when you open any other PowerPoint Presentation. To view your own theme, click the **Design** tab > **Themes** > **More** drop down; you can see the newly created theme under **Custom** section in the list.

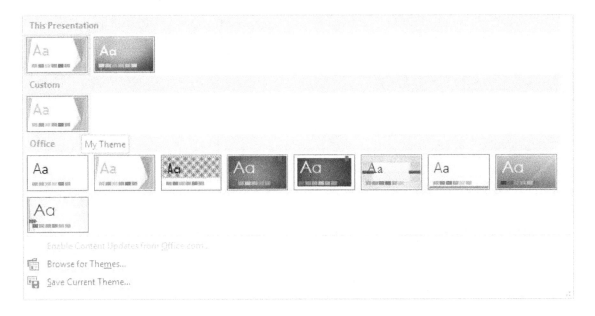

Creating Templates

PowerPoint allows you to save the settings of document as template for future use. To create your own template, first make sure that there is no content on the slides. Next, format the theme, color, text, and graphics. You can also divide the slides into sections if you want. After defining all the settings, follow the steps given next:

1. Click the **File** tab > **Save As** > **Browse** option (you can save on OneDrive or computer); the **Save As** dialog box appears.
2. Select the **PowerPoint Template** option from the **Save As Type** drop down.
3. Enter the **File Name**
4. Click the **Save** button.
5. Click the **Close** button to close the PowerPoint window.

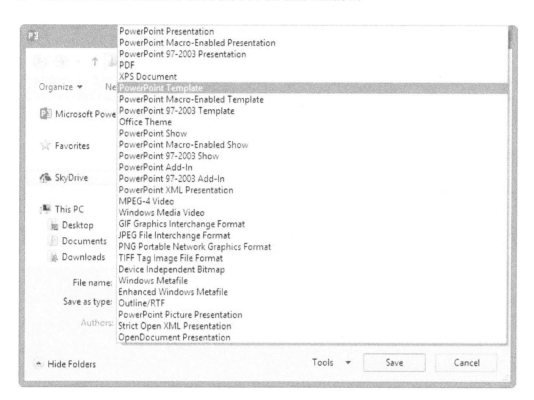

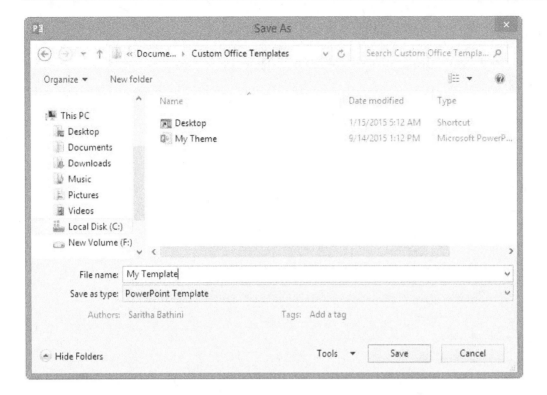

To start a new file using a custom template:

1. Open the PowerPoint Window.
2. Click the **Custom** option on the right-hand side and view the newly created template.
3. Click the **Custom Office Templates** folder.

4. Select the custom template.
5. Click the **Create** option to create a presentation.

Creating a Video

To create a Video of your presentation:

1. Click the **File** tab > **Export** > **Create a Video**; it opens the **Create a Video** page. In this page, you can see two options: **Presentation Quality** and **Recorded Timings and Narrations**.

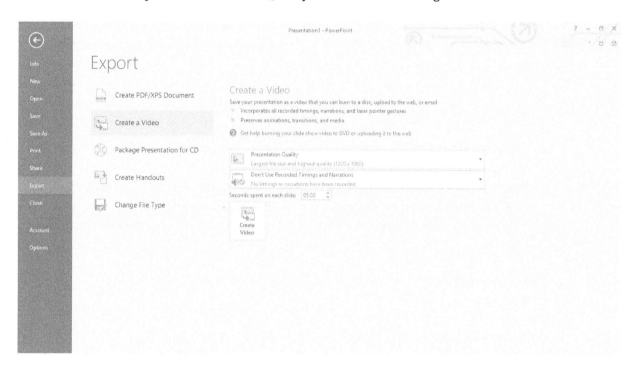

a. Select the **Presentation Quality** option to view the video on computer monitor or projector or high definition display. This option is useful for largest file size with high quality.

b. Select the **Internet Quality** option to upload the video to the web or burn to standard DVD. This option is useful for medium file size with standard quality.

c. Select the **Low Quality** option to view the video on a Portable device.

Note: It may display the text as small, which will be difficult to read but useful for small file size.

2. Select the **Use Recorded Timings and Narrations** option, if you have already recorded the Slide Show.

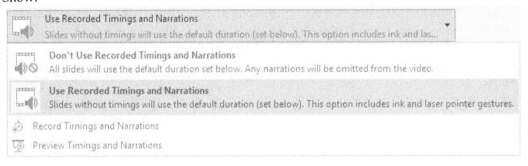

a. Select the **Don't Use Recorded Timings and Narrations** option, if you do not want the recorded timings and narrations.

b. Select the **Record Timings and Narrations** option, to record timings and narrations. It will record the presentation along with the timings and narrations.

c. Select the **Preview Timings and Narrations** option, to preview the recorded timing and narration.

3. Click the **Create Video** button to create a video; the **Save As** dialog box appears.

4. Set the **Save as type**.

5. Enter the file name.

6. Click the **Save** button; notice that the video is being created at the status bar.

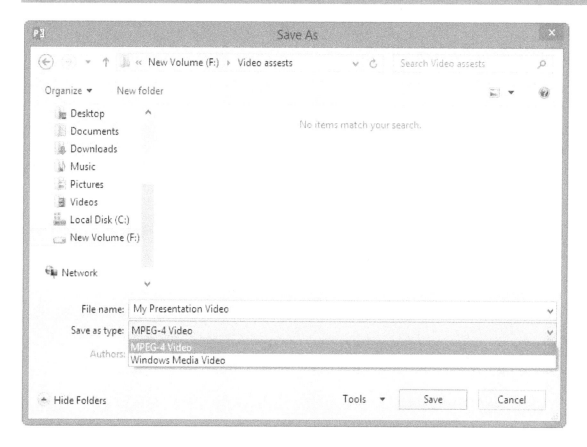

You can open the created video from the folder where you have saved.

Creating a PDF and JPEG File

PowerPoint allows you to convert a presentation into a PDF or JPEG file.

To create a PDF File:
1. Click the **File** tab > **Export** > **Create PDF/XPS Document**.
2. Click the **Create PDF/XPS** button in the **Create PDF/XPS Document** page; the **Publish as PDF or XPS** dialog box.

3. Select **Save as Type** drop down >**PDF**.
4. Enter the **File name**.
5. Make sure that the **Open file after publishing** option is selected to view the file after publishing.
6. Select **Optimize for** > **Minimum Size** to publish online. By default, the **Standard** size is selected, which is used to publish online and printing.
7. Click the **Options** button for more options; the **Options** dialog box appears.

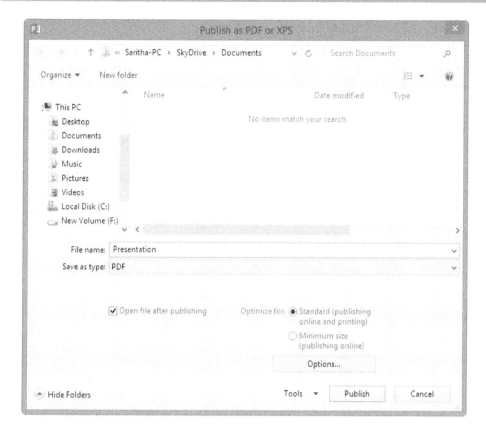

8. Select the slides to publish from the **Range** section.
9. Select what you want to publish from the **Publish what** drop down. You can select **Slides, Handouts, Notes Page**, and **Outline View**.

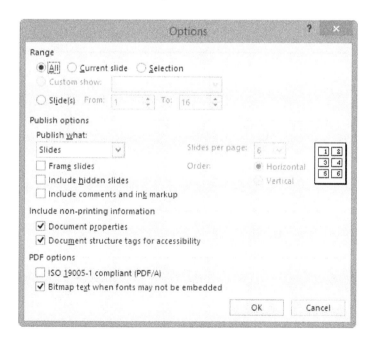

10. Select the **Frame Slides** check box to add **Frames** for slides.
11. Select the **Include Hidden Slides** checkbox to include hidden slides.
12. Select the **Include Comments and ink markup** checkbox to include comments and ink markup.
13. Click the **OK** button to apply.
14. Click the **Publish** button on the **Publish as PDF or XPS** dialog box to publish.

It may take few minutes to publish depending on the slides and graphics of your presentation.

After publishing, you can view the created PDF file by selecting it from the folder you have saved. By default, it opens after publishing.

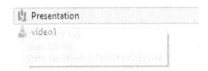

To create a JPEG file:
1. Select the slide that you want to convert into a jpeg file.
2. Click **File** tab > **Export**.
3. Click the **Change File Type > Image File Types > JPEG File Interchange Format**.

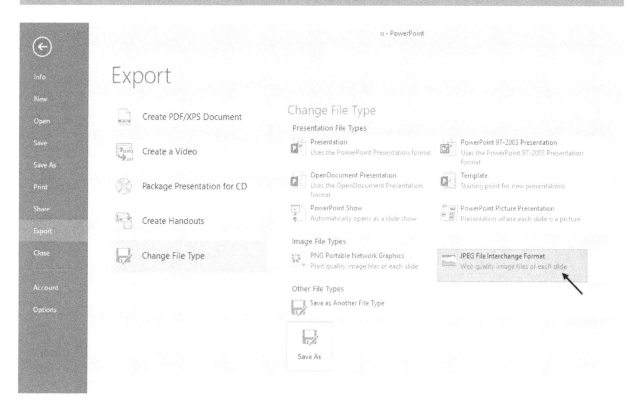

4. Click the **Save As** button; the **Save As** dialog box appears.
5. Select the folder where you want to save.
6. Click **Save as Type** drop down > **JPEG File Interchange Format**.
7. Enter the **File name**.
8. Click the **Save** button.

The **Microsoft PowerPoint dialog** prompts you to select the slides to export. click the **Just This One** button to save only the current slide as JPEG. click the **All Slides** button to save all slides as JPEG.

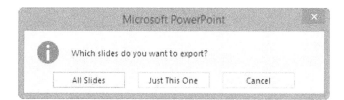

Sharing your Presentation
To send the presentation to any one of your colleagues:
1. Click the **File** tab > **Share** > **Email**; the **Email Page** appears.

2. Select the **Send as PDF** option to send the presentation as a PDF File; the **Microsoft Outlook** appears.
3. Enter the e-mail id in the **To** field.
4. Enter the subject in the **Subject** field.
5. Enter the body of the text.
6. Click the **Send** Button.

Similarly, you can send the presentation as an Attachment by clicking on the **Send as Attachment** option on the **Email Page**.

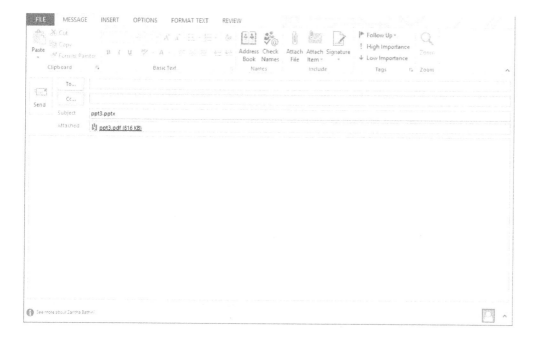

Inspecting for Comments

To inspect the document:

1. Click the **File** tab.
2. Click the **Info > Inspect Presentation > Check for Issues > Inspect Document**; the **Document Inspector** dialog box appears.

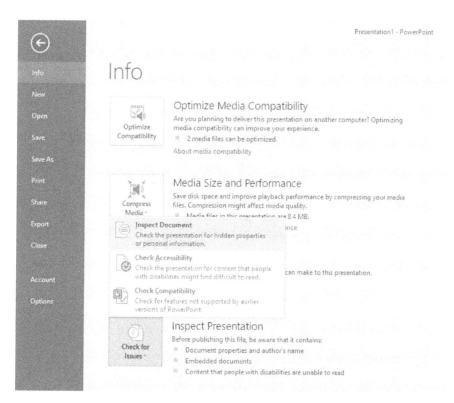

PowerPoint inspects for Comments and Annotations, Document Properties and Personal Information, Content Apps, Task Pane Apps, Custom Xml Data, Invisible On-Slide Content, off Slide Content, and Presentation Notes.

3. Click the **Inspect** button to inspect the document for selected content.
4. Click the **Remove all** button from the **Comments and Annotation** section, if you do not want to make any changes to the document.
5. Click the **Close** button on the dialog box.

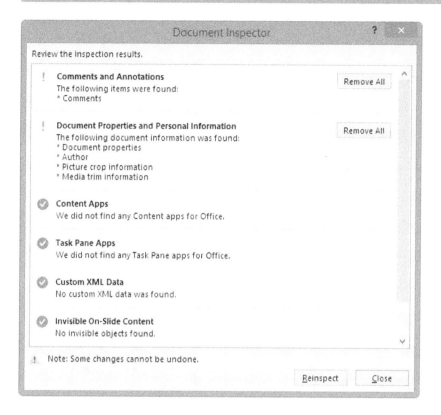

Protecting the Presentation

At some time, you may want to give access to your presentation only to specific people. You can give full permission (view and edit the presentation) or partial permission (only view) by assigning a password to the presentation.

There are two types of passwords:

Encrypted Password: This type of password locks the file completely. The people who do not know the password cannot open it.

Unencrypted Password: This type of password locks the file partially. The people who do not know the password cannot make changes to the presentation but they can open it in a read-only mode. However, they can edit and save it with a different name at a different location without effecting the original file.

Encrypted Password

To assign a password to your presentation:

1. Click the **File** tab > **Info** > **Protect Presentation** >**Encrypt with Password**; the **Encrypt Document** dialog box appears.
2. Type a password.
3. Click the **OK** button to apply.

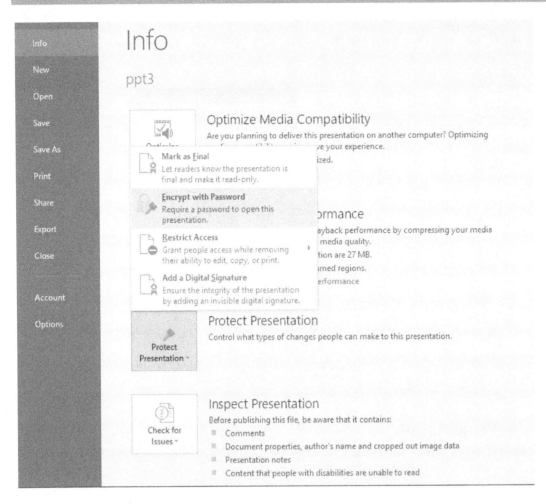

After assigning a password to the presentation, the **Password** dialog box appears when you try to open the presentation.

Enter the password to open the presentation and click the **OK** button to open the presentation.

To check whether the presentation is protected or not:
- Click **File** tab > **Info**; the **Protect Presentation** is highlighted stating that a password is required to open the presentation.

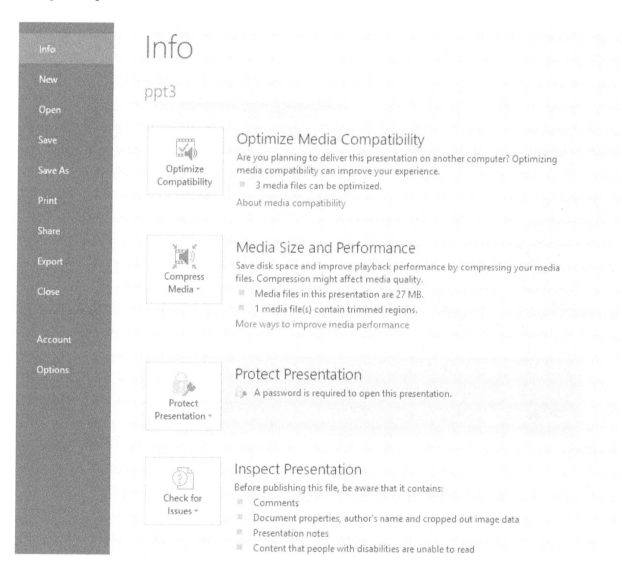

Unencrypted Password

To assign an unencrypted password:

1. Click **File tab** > **Info** > **Protect Presentation** > **Mark as Final**.
2. Click the **OK** button to apply.

Note: Remember that it is the final document and cannot make any changes to the presentation. The readers will view the presentation as a read-only and cannot edit it.

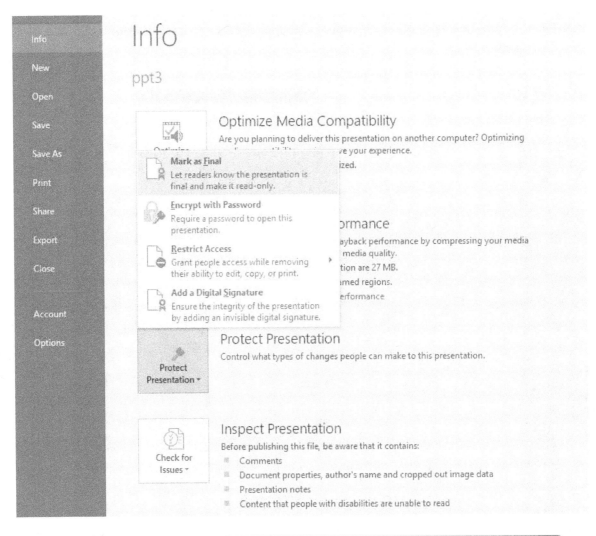

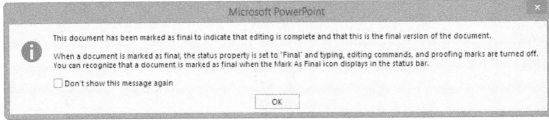

You can check whether the presentation is protected or not from the **File** tab. click **File** tab > **Info** and notice that the **Protect Presentation** is highlighted stating that the presentation has been marked as final to discourage editing.

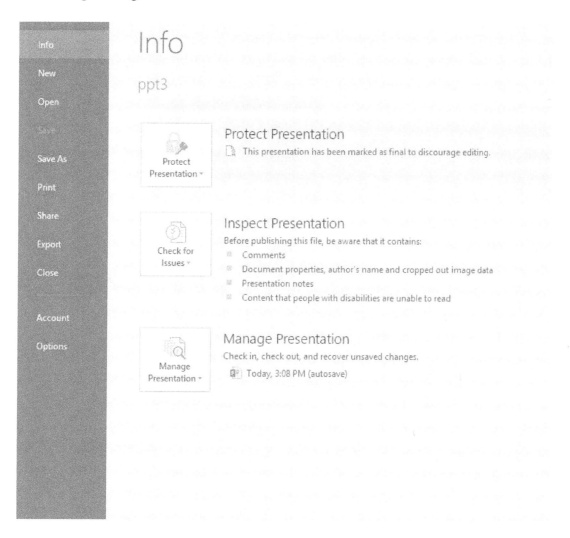

There are two more options in the **Protect Presentation** list, which help to protect the presentation: **Restrict Access** and **Add a Digital Signature**. You can click the **Restrict Access**, if your organization has implemented Information Rights Management (IRM). By selecting this option, the people can access the presentation to change, Print, or copy the presentation.

Click the **Add a Digital Signature** option, if you have a digital signature.

Index

www.ingramcontent.com/pod-product-compliance
Lightning Source LLC
LaVergne TN
LVHW060121070326
832902LV00019B/3073